Our Rich Root

Kingdom Promises for
The Kingdom Age

A Christocentric Interpretation
of the Prophets

An Apostolic Hermeneutic

Stan Newton

Our Rich Root

Kingdom Promises for the Kingdom Age

A Christocentric Interpretation of the Prophets

An Apostolic Hermeneutic

Stan Newton

Copyright © 2019 by Dr. Stan Newton

ISBN: 978-1-61529-211-0

Vision Publishing
P.O. Box 1680
Ramona, CA 92065
1-800-9-VISION
www.booksbyvision.org

"Unless otherwise indicated, all Scripture quotations are from the Holy Bible, English Standard Version, copyright 2001 by Crossway Bibles, a publishing ministry of Good News Publishers. Used by permission."

Cover Design by Lindsay Stefanov: lindsaystefanov.com

Endorsements

In my 40 years of full-time ministry, I have come across very few books with the wealth of information that is found in the pages of this book. Stan Newton has written a masterpiece that should be read by every serious student of the Word of God. Most believers today suffer from what I call identity crisis.

Believers today do not know who they are, and as a result do not know what they have as an inheritance. I deeply appreciate the Christ-centered message of this book. After all, He is the centerpiece of all creation. Apostle Paul said in the book of Galatians that the promise of inheritance was not made to seeds as of many, but to one seed, and to thy seed, which is Christ. And if you be Christ's, then are you Abraham's seed and heirs according to the promise. Do not be a victim of religious identity theft and forfeit your inheritance.

According to the book of Hebrews, without the death of the testator, the will is not effective. So, He wrapped himself in human flesh and died so you could get what is in the will. But more than that, He got back up from the dead to be the administrator of His own will to make sure we get our inheritance. As you read the pages of this book, your faith should reach out and lay hold of all the promises that God made to Abraham, our father of faith.

Lynn Hiles, Th.D., Ph.D.

Most of Jesus' teaching, and certainly the teaching of Paul and the other apostles, was rooted in Old Testament scriptures…refreshed, updated, and enhanced by the cross and resurrection of Christ. All of our theology and reading of scripture must be seen covenantally, that is, in light of the covenant of God with his people, and through the finished work of Christ.

We know that all scripture referred to in 2 Timothy 3:16 was from the Old Testament scriptures, and what God breathed upon still has life. It must be properly interpreted in light of the full revelation of Christ and all he has accomplished for us through his death, burial, ascension and enthronement. In this insightful book, *Our Rich Root*, the relevance of the Old Testament scripture for today is dissected and developed from the unique view and style of Dr. Stan Newton. As a professor of bible and theology, he presents his premises with clarity; it is well researched and powerfully presented. As a missionary with a pastor's heart, he elucidates the importance of knowing and loving the word of God...the whole word, and he embraces the prophetic proclamations of the Old Testament as vital for our walk in the Lord. This is a good read and it is relevant for today; it is revelatory and brilliantly presented.

Stan E. DeKoven, Ph.D.
President, Vision International University

So many Christians today have no clue what most O.T. prophecies speak about. Thus, we have the emergence of all the "personal revelation" type of interpretations. The book *Our Rich Root* is so vital because it clearly puts the prophetic words in their proper context - historically, as well as through the eyes of Jesus and His apostles.

I had long wondered who could write such a book, and I am more than pleased that it was Dr. Stan Newton. Using sound exegetical, hermeneutical, and eschatological methods of theology, this work is based on a Christo-centric approach. It will challenge your preconceived ideas and expand your boundaries.

Your vision for God's kingdom will grow and you will be on fire for new exploits as you experience the biblically fulness of what God has prepared for all of us. I warmly recommend this masterpiece.

Nikola Dimitrov
Pastor / Bible Teacher, Compiler of N.T. Wright endorsed:
The Four in One Gospel of Jesus

Stan Newton helps us see the relevance of the Old Testament prophets in light of the proclamation of the Kingdom of God, the gospel of Jesus and His Apostles. In particular, he helps us see the fulfillment of prophecy, as Christ builds His Church and the Kingdom through the church's manifestation on the earth. He deals with the related theological issues that come with the Kingdom understanding of the gospel. His work in this book warrants the attention of scholars and students alike.

Stan's understanding and explanation of the significance of the Olive Tree in scripture is more than worth the price of the book!"

Dr. Jim Bradshaw
President of Apostles Theological Seminary

"Stan Newton has done it again. Like his previous books Glorious Covenant and Glorious Kingdom, this book clears up confusion about which Covenant we are in and what the future holds for the church. And like his previous book, Breakfast in Tel Aviv, this book also deals with the issue of Israel and the church.

Because of this confusion, many Christians don't really know how to read the Old Testament, but that was not always the case. In previous generations, believers drew great strength from the Old Testament, seeing it as speaking of Christ and our life in Christ and the advancing of the Kingdom of Christ. Stan puts this best in one section where he says:

"Not everything written in the Old Testament is Old Covenant. There is a large amount of New Covenant promises written in the Old Testament. The prophet Joel is a good example. His well-known prophecy that the Holy Spirit would be poured out was fulfilled in the followers of Jesus at Pentecost. We have a prophecy. We have its fulfillment. Over, right? Well, no, it's not over; it was just the beginning. While the day of Pentecost was the fulfill-

ment of Joel's prophecy, it was the start of a whole new age of the Spirit for the followers of Jesus. It was not the end. So, we have a fulfillment of a word from an Old Testament Prophet and then we see it continually fulfilled in the church. This is the pattern in a multitude of Old Testament passages."

If you are looking for a book which shows a wide sweep of scripture throughout the Old and New Testaments; one that shows the continuity of passages and how God is working His plan throughout history; a book to give you a secure grounding in God's Advancing Kingdom; then this is that book.

Dr. Martin Trench
Author, Teacher, Apostolic Consultant and Lead Pastor of
Gateway Church, Edmonton, Alberta, Canada

Our Rich Root will steer the reader to the correct historical and contextual conclusion to bring the body of Christ fully into kingdom advancement. Dr. Stan Newton gently leads the reader by examining scriptures to establish the truth of our roots; by linking our theology, including covenant and eschatology, to the fulfillment of prophecy. We are not to ignore the Old Testament but search for Jesus in every book in order to catapult the believer into deep revelation by the Holy Spirit's illumination. This book delivers what is in Stan's heart to reach a rich conclusion.

Col 2:7 "Have the roots [of your being] firmly and deeply planted [in Him, fixed and founded in Him], being continually built up in Him, becoming increasingly more confirmed and established in the faith, just as you were taught, and abounding and overflowing in it with thanksgiving."

Patricia Garitson, Pastor at Solid Rock Church, Sedona, AZ
Kingdom Revivalist

Shapeyourdestinyimage.com
www.solidrockchurchofsedona.com/youTube channel carlsedona

Our Rich Root is one of the finest expositions on Romans 11 available to us today. Stan's exhaustive and clear understanding of The Olive Tree and how it relates to the church, is outstanding. His interpretation of Old Testament Prophets is one of the clearest explanations of God's Kingdom in print. He has been able to put the Old Testament prophecies into the proper perspective for today's church. He takes us to Jesus and the New Testament writers. He shows their understanding and perspective of the Old Testament, and how it relates to the Kingdom of God. The result is that we begin to understand our "rich root" found in the Old Testament.

Stan helps us unravel the Old Testament kingdom promises and how they prophetically apply to today's church. When we see the words of the prophets applied to the advancing Kingdom of God through the New Testament writers, then our vision and revelation of the church is encouraged and advanced.

I believe this book will become a foundational work. It will strengthen the church and help to dispel the theological errors that have hindered the expansion of God's Kingdom.

We are truly fortunate to have a man of Stan's integrity and spiritual understanding leading us into a fuller revelation of God's "Advancing Kingdom."

Robert Young, Retired Pastor

Dr. Stan Newton has done it again! With detailed accuracy he tackles kingdom theology from an academic stand point and lays out biblical arguments for the present reign of Christ and His kingdom. In Our Rich Root Dr Newton gives us a Christocentric model of interpretation of scripture showing in great detail that the Prophets of the Old Testament looked forward into our day and saw the Church (Believers in Christ) as those living in and advancing His kingdom from the ascension and coronation of Christ until His return! Our Rich Root is a must read for any serious student of eschatology, and any believer who wants to understand the Church's mission on this earth. Acts 3:21 whom heaven must receive until the times of restoration of all things, which God has spoken by the mouth of all His holy prophets since the world began.

Charles Seip, Senior Leader Higher Ground Worship Center,
Nampa Idaho

When Stan Newton asked me to read his new manuscript, *Our Rich Root,* I was excited because I had already read one of Stans other books called *The Glorious Kingdom* and I felt that that book was making a significant contribution for the understanding of the end times or Eschatology.

So, I was anticipating what Stan would say in this new book and I was not disappointed.

John 5:39 is a powerful verse "You search the Scriptures because you think that in them you have eternal life; it is these that testify about Me;" NAS. Obviously the people of Jesus's day and the people today think that that is exactly what the Bible is. Jesus is making it very clear that that is not the purpose of the scriptures. The purpose of the scriptures is to reveal who Jesus is, what He has done and the impact it has on every living soul. He himself is eternal life. Stan takes this verse and many others and helps us form a truly form an Apostolic and hermeneutic that is truly inclusive of both the new and old Testaments and lets us understand how Jesus's very Apostles were concluding about His work and also how they continued to receive revelation through the Holy writ.

I congratulate Stan on this new book and once again I feel he has made another significant contribution of growth and development to the body of Christ.

Dr. Richard H. Hays
Director and founder of Christian Community International

Table of Contents

Preface

This book was birthed out of a perceived necessity. If the arguments and conclusions found here are wrong or in need of correction, hopefully that will spur more discussion of this vital subject. The necessity for me was to challenge the church and avoid a major pitfall in our kingdom theology; namely, to rip the Old Testament out of our consideration.

This can happen in two ways. First, for several generations dispensational theology has made the prophecies of the Old Testament void, by stealing them from the true people of the kingdom - the church; and assigning them to a future age - the 1,000-year millennium. The second problem is a conviction that everything was fulfilled in Christ. Why is this a problem? If the words of the Prophets cannot be applied to the advancing kingdom of God, in and through the church, we lose a great treasure of prophetic word. The church must be built upon a foundation of hope and that foundation is first found in the Old Testament Prophets. Both positions are inconsistent with what the apostolic authors of the New Testament wrote and declared as central to the Christian faith.

I will restate my conviction. I am not backtracking on my conclusions in *Glorious Covenant*; one-hundred percent of the old covenant is obsolete and no longer has any binding authority over the church. Yet, there is a major difference between saying that the old covenant is no longer valid and saying the entire Old Testament has become obsolete. The entire Old Testament is useful and needed. We will make a mistake if we conclude the entire Old Testament is the old covenant.

The old covenant is the Mosaic Law. There are portions of Scripture in the Old Testament, especially in the prophets, that speak to the new covenant and the present kingdom of God. When seen through the finished work of Christ, these passages add vision and revelation to the church as we advance the kingdom of God on the earth. They reveal where we are going. They are more than helpful; they are necessary.

Our Rich Root will be divided into two sections. The first section will address foundational issues, which are more theological in nature. The second will be a sampling of Old Testament prophecies and how they can be applied to the church. The second section is more exegetical.

Section I
Theological and Practical Importance of the Old Testament Prophets

Chapter 1
Locating Our Missing Inheritance

But if some of the branches were broken off, and you, being a wild olive, were grafted in among them and became partaker with them of the rich root of the olive tree. (Romans 11:17 NASB)

You are the sons of the prophets and of the covenant that God made with your fathers, saying to Abraham, 'And in your offspring shall all the families of the earth be blessed (Acts 3:25).

Finding a lost inheritance is exciting. Discovering a place where heaping treasures of kingdom promises may be found is equally exciting. Yet, there are many biblical treasures that remain 'unmined' by the church. They are in our Bible, and for the most part these Old Testament passages are either unknown or undervalued. What is missing is the understanding of the connection between these prophetic revelations and the kingdom of Jesus.

We have been robbed. Tradition and denominational doctrines have buried our inheritance. It is still there, but layers of ecclesiastical dust must first be removed. This is our challenge. The advancement of God's kingdom on earth will be more effective, when we draw upon the 'rich root' of the Hebrew Prophets.

The Bible is our foundation and blueprint for discipling the nations. And that same Bible includes both Testaments, the New and the Old. Our desire is to see the knowledge of the Glory of God cover the earth. Therefore, we cannot throw away a large portion of God's inspired word without dumbing down our revelation of the kingdom.

Understanding the new covenant is necessary to rid us of the legalism of religion, but the problem of legalism is not solved by eliminating the Old Testament. We must still see the word of the prophets as foundational to our kingdom vision. The Old Testament is more than a history of Israel; it is the 'rich root' of God's promises for the church.

Who are the Prophets in the Old Testament? They can be divided in two periods. The first group began with Samuel and ended with John the Baptist. The second group began with the Ascension of Christ (Ephesians 4:10-11) and continues until the church reaches maturity - the fullness of Christ. These Prophets are a gift to the church from Christ, as they minister to God's new covenant people.

The church drew strength from the writings of the Old Testament Prophets for centuries. They were viewed as God's orators to reveal his purpose and dreams. The New Testament apostles and leaders found fresh revelation in the Old Testament. Their understanding of the Messiah and his kingdom was enhanced as they used their 'apostolic' discernment to gain insight into how the 'prophetic passages' in the Old Testament were to be understood. They read themselves into the story. And this is exactly what we should do. We are not a forgotten people. We belong to the fresh revelation of Israel's Messiah and his new people; the church. Isaiah, Amos, Jeremiah, Zechariah and the other Prophets were seen by the church not only as men who spoke to old covenant Israel, but also as voices for the new thing God would do once the Messiah had come. They were Prophets of the Kingdom.

It is interesting how often the authors of the New Testament quote passages from the Old Testament. That should not be surprising, because the Old Testament was their only Scripture. Those of us who listened to the music of Simon and Garfunkel may remember that the "Words of the Prophets are written on the subway walls." Yet, the best place to read the words of the Prophets is in the Hebrew Scriptures. The early church had one inspired Scripture - the Old Testament.

There are different ways to interpret the Old Testament. We have large portions dealing with Israel's history, as well as passages like Proverbs and Psalms, which provide inspiration for worship and wisdom for practical living. Then there are those passages, which have prophetic meaning. They can be divided three ways. First, words for Israel and Judah that are limited to a specific time and place. Second, prophecies finding their fulfillment in the birth of or some other event in the ministry of Jesus. These are not to be repeated. There will never be another birth of the Messiah. Jesus will never again die on the cross or be resurrected. His baptism and other single events will not be repeated. The Prophets of Israel proclaimed these events hundreds of years before they happened. Third, prophetic words which are fulfilled in and through the church in the kingdom.

We can stop looking for future fulfillments of those Messianic prophecies which point to single events in the life of Jesus. Yet there are also words from the Prophets that spoke a lot about the kingdom and about a different type of covenant; these words coincide with the coming of the Messiah. It is these specific kingdom prophecies which need further exploration.

This is the missing link in our understanding of the depth and beauty of the kingdom age in which we are living. Actually, that is the debatable point. Do we live in the age of the kingdom? Is the kingdom we are living in the fulfillment of what the Prophets saw? Or are we living, as the dispensationalists claim, in a different kingdom, a mystery kingdom which is not spoken of or seen by the Prophets?

We must address several presumptions here. One, the doctrinal system of dispensationalism has robbed the church by disallowing any words from the Old Testament Prophets to be applied to the church. Dispensational eschatology divides the people of God into separate groups; Israel and the church. Jesus came as Israel's Messiah and was rejected by his own people. Therefore, the kingdom was 'postponed' until the Second Coming, when Israel will accept its Messiah and see the fulfillment of the promises spoken through the prophets.

According to the dispensational system, the church is not seen or spoken of throughout the Old Testament. The church was a mystery until the time of Jesus, so it is separated from every promise of the prophets. There are Messianic prophecies, but they all refer to Jesus as an individual; none are for the church. Nothing has robbed the church more than this doctrine. The church is reduced to God's plan 'B' and natural Israel is the primary people group God desires to work through.

The second presumption has several layers of thought. The first is, "Christ fulfilled all Old Testament promises." A similar one goes like this, "Those promises are old covenant." I agree that the Messianic and kingdom promises and covenants (like the Abrahamic and Davidic ones) come through Jesus. Nothing occurs in biblical prophecy without Jesus at the center of its fulfillment.

Apostle Paul understood that all the promises were *Yes* in Christ (II Corinthians 1:20). Yet the reason Christ fulfills everything is so we may walk in it. The promises are not abolished. Christ fulfills them, so we can experience them. We will need a different word than *fulfilled*, if we would like to say: *no longer useful or needed*. Or, maybe we can say they are fulfilled, but not yet completed. Either way, we must move beyond the thinking that everything is over, because it is not. We are at the beginning of seeing the promises of God being *fulfilled* or *brought to completion* on the earth. So, where do we find this rich resource of kingdom promises? In the Old Testament Prophets.

It should not surprise us that kingdom promises have their fulfillment in the age of the kingdom.

Dispensational eschatology correctly understands that Old Testament kingdom promises are to be fulfilled in the age of the kingdom. Where they get it horribly wrong is placing the kingdom age into our future. By separating the church from the kingdom, they create a theology where all Old Testament kingdom promises are 'postponed' until the Second Coming and the millennial kingdom.

We live in the age of the kingdom. It began with Jesus and his ministry on earth over 2,000 years ago. Since the kingdom is now, what should be done with the large quantity of prophecies in the Old Testament which speak to God's work when the Messiah would come? Should we dismiss these as 'Already fulfilled in Christ', or ignore them because we think they are "old covenant?" If this is our choice, we are neglecting our inheritance. We are forsaking a rich deposit of prophetic words which the church needs. We can do better. We must do better!

Not everything written in the Old Testament is old covenant.

There is a large amount of new covenant promises written in the Old Testament. The prophet Joel is a good example. His well-known prophecy that the Holy Spirit would be poured out was fulfilled in the followers of Jesus at Pentecost. We have a prophecy. We have its fulfillment. Over, right? Well, no, it's not over; it was just the beginning. While the day of Pentecost was the fulfillment of Joel's prophecy, it was the start of a whole new age of the outpouring of the Spirit for the followers of Jesus. It was not the end. So, we have a fulfillment of a word from an Old Testament Prophet and then we see it continually fulfilled in the church. This is the pattern in a multitude of Old Testament passages.

Jesus is the only one who went to the cross and rose from the dead. He is the only Messiah so, yes, all the Law and the Prophets speak of him. Yet his body, the new covenant church, finds fulfillment in these prophecies as well.

Another example is found in Isaiah. He saw in the future and prophesied new covenant truth.

For the earth will be filled with the knowledge of the LORD *as the waters cover the sea.* (Isaiah 11:9)

There may be no other verse in the entire Bible that more effectively captures our imaginations and releases our dreams for a better world. We dream of a world where righteousness, peace and joy fill our cities and the surrounding countryside. This is the world that Jesus died for; a world where God has a family that is sharing his love and grace to all creation. A people on earth who live with purpose, joy and adventure. I believe this has been the desire of God from the beginning. A few hundred years after Isaiah, another Prophet repeated the promise but in a slightly different manner. This promise provides a generational hope for the church. It begins with the incarnation of Jesus and continues now through his kingship.

For the earth will be filled with the knowledge of the glory of the LORD as the waters cover the sea. (Habakkuk 2:14)

I believe the glory of God does fill the earth now. The problem is that far too many people are not aware of it. When God's people walk in the *"knowledge of the glory"*, others will begin to desire and walk in it too. This is a prophecy made possible through the work of Christ and is now progressively being fulfilled.

This promise from God was not completely fulfilled at the cross. Actually, it was the cross that made it possible.

The question now is one of proper exegesis and hermeneutics. Can we apply this promise to the church? Or is this another example of the many promises left unfulfilled because Israel broke the covenant? If we claim it is for Israel in the future, we join the dispensationalists and have no real faith for the church. If we say, "Since it is an Old Testament promise, it has now been fulfilled in Christ", the result is no different. Both positions rob the church of her destiny.

What would be a sound approach in taking this promise and applying it to the church and our future? In chapters 4 and 5 we will examine two methods of interpretation, which I believe will be of great help in returning these great promises of the prophets back to the church. For too long we have been told, "These promises and covenants are not for us." It is time to claim our inheritance. Before launching into hermeneutics, we have Apostle Paul's image of the "olive tree" to discuss. This image and the theology behind it are the central truths that we will build around.

It is time to view the Old Testament through the lens of Christ and apply the theology of the new covenant in our exegesis of the prophets. This will reveal the heart of what God is saying to us and provide the church with a rich deposit of promises and principles for the advancing kingdom we are living in.

Where should we begin? In his letter to the Romans, apostle Paul is using the symbol of an olive tree to make a profound theological statement. That would be a good place to start.

Chapter 2
The Olive Tree

Apostle Paul writes an extensive statement of faith in the book of Romans, which includes the connection between Israel and the church. In chapter 11 he uses the olive tree to show what has happened to Israel since the cross.

In the natural, the olive tree is a very strong tree. It is drought and fire resistant. Why? Because it has a 'robust root system.' The olive tree, "Is very hardy, due to its drought, disease, and fire resistance. In large part, this is due to its extensive and robust root system, that is capable of regenerating itself even if the trunk is destroyed by fire. Consequently, it can and does live a very long time. Some olive trees in the Mediterranean area have been estimated to be 2,000 years of age; most are hundreds of years of age".[1] I believe the natural strength and longevity of the olive tree exemplifies the strong 'spiritual' connection between Israel and the church.

It is the 'spiritual value' of this "robust root system" that I wish to explore. It is my conviction it contains needed spiritual nourishment and revelation that the church needs badly; the revelation of the kingdom of God.

What does the olive tree represent? What should be obvious is often made overly complex. Paul has three groups in mind. First, the tree itself is Israel. Second, branches were broken off from the tree; these are the individual Jews, who rejected the Messiah. A *third* group, which were branches from a wild olive tree, were grafted in; which would be the Gentile believers. Then we have the root system of the tree, which represents the covenants and promises of the family of Abraham. Jeremiah spoke of Israel as being an "olive tree" in the context of being judged and being conquered by Babylon.

---

[1] Stuart H. Pouliot, ttp://www.kingdomandglory.com/art/art34.html

The LORD once called you 'a green olive tree, beautiful with good fruit.' But with the roar of a great tempest he will set fire to it, and its branches will be consumed. (Jeremiah 11:16)

In the time of Jeremiah, the *"green olive tree"* was destroyed by Babylon. The branches were destroyed, but not the 'root.' Paul may have had this in mind when he began writing about the olive tree in Romans 11. When Jeremiah wrote this, Israel was in rebellion and therefore facing a terrible judgment. Jeremiah declared, *"its branches will be consumed."* Is this what Paul had in mind when, generations later, Israel faced a similar situation? Their day had come, and the majority of Israel would not believe. Therefore, those who were in 'unbelief' were like branches of an olive tree that were removed. The olive tree was Israel. It was the family of God directly related to Abraham.

Jesus might have had Jeremiah's words in mind as well, when he taught about the 'true vine.' *"If anyone does not abide in me he is thrown away like a branch and withers; and the branches are gathered, thrown into the fire, and burned"* (John 15:6).

So, what is the "Olive Tree?"

N.T. Wright: "So, what is the 'olive tree'? It is, of course, a metaphor for Israel itself."[2]

The olive tree traces the history of a family; the family of Abraham. This is the root system which is extensive and secure. It includes the covenants given to Abraham and David, as well as Jeremiah's prophecy of the new covenant. It includes the words of the prophets. It includes comprehensive promises given to Israel.

Albert Barnes: "Partakers of the root - The engrafted limb would derive nourishment from the root, as though it were a natural branch of the tree. The Gentiles now derived the benefit of Abraham's faith and holy labors, and of the promises made to him and to his seed.

---

[2] N.T. Wright, Paul And The Faithfulness of God, Fortress Press, Minneapolis, 2013, page 1213

Fatness of the olive-tree - The word "fatness" here means "fertility, fruitfulness" - the rich juices of the olive producing fruit."[3]

Barnes makes an excellent point that Gentiles who are grafted into the olive tree have the same rights and benefits as those originally part of the tree. There is no longer any separation between Jews and Gentiles once they have been grafted into the tree.

Expositor's Bible Commentary: "Union with Christ was union with Abraham."

ICC New Testament Commentary: "The image of an olive tree to describe Israel is taken from the Prophets", Jeremiah 11:16."[4]

Besides the use of the 'olive tree' Apostle Paul used other metaphors to express the same concept.

Ephesians 2: 12 Gentiles are included in the *"Commonwealth of Israel."*

Ephesians 2:15 Believing Jews and believing Gentiles are now *"One new man."*

Galatians 3:29 Believing Gentiles are *"Abraham's offspring"* and *"heirs."*

Galatians 6:16 Those who are part of the *"New Creation"* are called the *"Israel of God."*

Charles P. Schmitt: "In every sense of the word, the apostolic church had its roots in the richness of the corporate Israel of God of the Old Testament."[5]

N.T. Wright: "Israel as an olive tree is a familiar biblical image, often in a positive and attractive sense. The whole point of the image is that there is - just as in Galatians 3 - a single family; a family

---

[3] Albert Barnes, https://biblehub.com/commentaries/barnes/romans/11.htm

[4] ICC New Testament Commentary, https://biblehub.com/commentaries/icc/romans/11.htm

[5] Charles P. Schmitt, Floods Upon the Dry Grounds, Revival Press-Destiny Image Publishers, Shippensburg, PA. page 2vf

rooted in the patriarchs and the promises God made to them; a family from which, strangely, many 'natural branches' have been broken off, but into which many 'unnatural branches' have been grafted. This is the family Paul has been talking about, on and off, throughout the letter, not least in chapter 4. This is the people into which some Gentiles have surprisingly been brought and from which some Jews have surprisingly opted out, as in 9:30-10:13. There ought to be no further question about this: Paul is talking about the ancient people of God, now radically reconfigured around the Messiah."[6]

Wright makes an important point, when he says there is a single family of God, "A family rooted in the patriarchs and the promises of God." The patriarchs like Abraham and David, with their covenants and the promises spoken by the prophets, provide the church with vision for a better future. Wright mentions Galatians 3, where Paul once again makes a case for Gentiles to be included in the rich root of the family of Abraham.

Christ redeemed us from the curse of the law by becoming a curse for us—for it is written, "Cursed is everyone who is hanged on a tree" — so that in Christ Jesus the blessing of Abraham might come to the Gentiles, so that we might receive the promised Spirit through faith. (Galatians 3:13-14)

Paul brings up two factors, which are part of the 'blessing of Abraham.' First, we can receive the promised Holy Spirit, and second, this Spirit is received through faith. We cannot ignore the central role of the Holy Spirit in causing us to partake of the Abrahamic family and its blessings.

The first group represented by the olive tree is Israel. This is national Israel, the people of the old covenant. Then, Paul writes that branches were broken off. These were individual Jews, who rejected Jesus as their Messiah. What took many by surprise was that the conditions to 'remain Israel" changed with the arrival of their

---

[6] Ibid.

Messiah. Those 'of Israel', who rejected their own Messiah, were removed from being a part of the people of God. They lost their inheritance. This is supported by the words of Jesus in the gospel of Matthew.

Therefore, I tell you, the kingdom of God will be taken away from you and given to a people producing its fruits. (Matthew 21:43)

Large sections of the New Testament attest to a coming judgment upon unbelieving Israel. This came into reality when Jerusalem was destroyed along with the temple, in 70 A.D.

For you, brothers, became imitators of the churches of God in Christ Jesus that are in Judea. For you suffered the same things from your own countrymen as they did from the Jews, who killed both the Lord Jesus and the prophets, and drove us out, and displease God and oppose all mankind by hindering us from speaking to the Gentiles that they might be saved—so as always to fill up the measure of their sins. But wrath has come upon them at last! (I Thessalonians 2:14-16)

This was written approximately 12-14 years before the Romans came, burned the temple and destroyed the city. This was more than a political disaster; it was the judgment of God. Why did Paul state the wrath of God was about to be poured out on these first-century Jews? Because their sin had come to its full. These were the 'broken branches' in Romans 11.

We must recognize the fact that not all accept Paul's image of the olive tree to be Israel. Dispensationalists and their doctrine that the Old Testament says nothing, sees nothing and prophesies nothing concerning the church, go to great lengths to avoid what Paul is clearly stating.

C.I. Scofield (A Dispensational position): "Israel is judicially broken off from the good olive tree, Christ."[7]

---

[7] C.I Scofield, Scofield's Reference Notes, Romans 11

Dispensationalism must at all cost keep the church separate from Israel and away from the words of the Old Testament Prophets. If they interpret the olive tree as Christ, they can maintain the discontinuity of Israel and the church. Yet, the major point Paul is making by the olive tree is there is 'one family of Abraham'. Continuity is the key.

If natural Israel was the olive tree and unbelieving Jews were the branches broken off, who was the 'wild olive shoot' that was grafted in?" It was the Gentiles, who came to faith in Jesus.

But if some of the branches were broken off, and you, although a wild olive shoot, were grafted in among the others and now share in the nourishing root of the olive tree. (Romans 11:17)

Gentiles were added into the olive tree. It is still the same olive tree, with deep roots in the Old Testament promises, yet, the tree is somehow different as well. It has been pruned. It has been cut back by the removal of many branches. It is not close to death, though, because of its recent 'radical trimming.' Other branches are grafted in. Gentiles, who have turned to Christ, are now included and can draw from the rich root, which are the covenants and promises given to Israel.

The words of the Prophets about a coming Messiah and his kingdom are part of the new covenant promises. Different versions of this passage bring out a fresh look.

ESV: We share in the "*nourishing root*" of the olive tree.

NKJV: It says we "*became a partaker of the root and fatness of the olive tree.*"

The Living Bible: "*But some of these branches from Abraham's tree, some of the Jews, have been broken off. And you Gentiles who were branches from, we might say, a wild olive tree, were grafted in. So now you, too, receive the blessing God has promised Abraham and his children, sharing in God's rich nourishment of his own special olive tree.*

The Passion Translation: *However, some of the branches have been pruned away. And you, who were once nothing more than a wild olive branch in the desert, God has grafted in—inserting you among the remaining branches as a joint partner to share in the wonderful richness of the cultivated olive stem.*

We are a *"joint partner"'* of the *"wonderful richness"* of God's tree. We are not separated from them, but because of the new covenant, we can see their true spiritual fulfillment. If our vision for the kingdom needs to be enlarged, then we should begin to draw from the rich root.

Gentiles are grafted into the olive tree with its rich and nourishing root system. The church does not exist out of nothing. We have deep and rich roots, which are the glorious kingdom promises spoken of by the Hebrew Prophets. Our roots go back to Abraham and the covenant God made with him (Galatians 3:28-29). Our roots extend back to David and the promise of a world-wide kingdom (Acts 2:29-30). We have deep roots in the tree of Israel.

If unbelieving Israel was not a part of the olive tree we were grafted into, then, what people are we grafted into? Paul answered that earlier in chapter 11.

I ask, then, has God rejected his people? By no means! For I myself am an Israelite, a descendant of Abraham, a member of the tribe of Benjamin. God has not rejected his people whom he foreknew. Do you not know what the Scripture says of Elijah, how he appeals to God against Israel? "Lord, they have killed your prophets, they have demolished your altars, and I alone am left, and they seek my life." But what is God's reply to him? "I have kept for myself seven thousand men who have not bowed the knee to Baal." So too at the present time there is a remnant, chosen by grace. But if it is by grace, it is no longer on the basis of works; otherwise grace would no longer be grace. What then? Israel failed to obtain what it was seeking. The elect obtained it, but the rest were hardened. (Romans 11:1-7)

Has God rejected Israel because the majority did not believe? Paul says, "No!" Why? First, because Paul himself was a believer, as well as many other Jews. Therefore, this remnant continued to be the recipient of the "rich root" of the olive tree. Also, those who have rejected the Messiah and the new covenant could at a later point be grafted back in. God will not give up on people. If the unbelieving Jews of the first century were 'rejected' by God, then, there would be no place for repentance and restoration.

Gentiles were grafted into the first-century Jewish believers. These Jewish believers were the first-fruits and heirs of all the promises and covenants of God. True, all of this looks different when it is viewed from a new covenant perspective, yet, that is our task; to see how these covenants and promises of the prophets are to be understood. Second, if God had rejected Israel, then all the promises, the Abrahamic covenant and the words of the prophets would no longer have any value. If they have no meaning, what then, would be the purpose of being grafted into the 'rich root' of the olive tree?

I find it interesting that Paul's argument in Romans 11 starts with the statement that God has not rejected his people (old covenant Israel). Then, in verse 15 he writes, *"For if their rejection means the reconciliation of the world..."* How can it be both ways? It can, because of what Paul explains earlier; Israel is not rejected because of the remnant. As an old covenant nation, Israel has been rejected, because of their unbelief.

What about the Jews who were cut off from the olive tree? Was there any hope? Yes, under the new covenant all were welcome. At any time, anyone, of any ethnic background, could be added. Jews today are not under any type of curse or judgment; that ended in the fall of 70 AD. All through history they have had the same open door to hear and respond to the gospel, as anyone else. The offer is always open.

For if you were cut from what is by nature a wild olive tree, and grafted, contrary to nature, into a cultivated olive tree, how much more will these, the natural branches, be grafted back into their own olive tree. (Roman 11:24)

Apostle Paul warns the Gentiles who were grafted in, not to become proud of their status; because God could graft Jews back into the tree. Our prayer is for those from the natural bloodline of Abraham to be added back into God's olive tree. The path is clear; it is through their Messiah - Jesus.

Since we are grafted into the 'remnant' of Israel, we have legal rights to all that was promised. Therefore, our New Testament theology should include an explanation of how the covenants and promises work in and for the members of the church. We cannot allow this rich deposit of promises to be stolen by dispensationalism or ignored as being 'old covenant.'

Here is more about the olive tree and its branches: "The olive branch has been a symbol for a very long time and not just for those in the Bible. In the 5th century BC, the Greeks were already using it as a symbol of peace. In biblical accounts, extending an olive branch meant the ending of hostilities between two parties and signaled the end of the conflict. The United Nations' flag contains an olive branch for this very purpose; to end all hostilities between warring nations or those facing confrontation, but it's also found on many of the nations' symbols, like in the 1885 Great Seal of the United States." [8]

The olive branch symbol is one of peace. The peace everyone desires is found only in the work of Jesus by creating a new people. *"And he came and preached peace to you who were far off and peace to those who were near. For through him we both have access in one Spirit to the Father (Ephesians 2:17-18).*

---

[8] https://www.whatchristianswanttoknow.com/what-does-the-olive-tree-or-olive-branch-symbolize-in-the-bible/#ixzz50egHtlLj)

Abundant Fruit

The purpose for having a robust root system is to produce an abundant harvest of quality fruit. When we erase our understanding of the Old Testament prophets, we diminish the root system and therefore the fruit of the church is also diminished. Jesus and the apostles spoke often about fruit and its application to our spiritual lives.

Bear fruits in keeping with repentance. And do not begin to say to yourselves, 'We have Abraham as our father.' For I tell you, God is able from these stones to raise up children for Abraham. Even now the axe is laid to the root of the trees. Every tree therefore that does not bear good fruit is cut down and thrown into the fire. (Luke 3:8-9)

Our repentance should bear fruit. In context, we read that many first-century Jews were claiming, "Abraham is our Father" as an excuse for rejecting Jesus as their Messiah. They were saying to Jesus, "We do not need you, we have Abraham." Within this context, their "fruit" would be their 'change of minds' concerning Jesus. Belief would have been the fruit of their repentance.

Either make the tree good and its fruit good, or make the tree bad and its fruit bad, for the tree is known by its fruit. (Matthew 12:33)

The easiest way to determine what kind of fruit tree you have is to pick its fruit. Those working in orchards can tell by the shape or color of the leaves, the color and texture of the bark, but for the rest of us, the tree is known by the type of fruit it produces. The fruit comes from the type of person we are. Jesus is giving people a choice here. Be a good tree or a bad one. The choice we make will be known to all by the type of fruit being produced.

You did not choose me, but I chose you and appointed you that you should go and bear fruit and that your fruit should abide, so that whatever you ask the Father in my name, he may give it to you. (John 15:16)

We are not only called to bear fruit, but we need fruit that endures. If we died today, would there be fruit that continues to glorify God and bless others? What about our local churches? Are we producing generational fruit or only blessings for the season?

Likewise, my brothers, you also have died to the law through the body of Christ, so that you may belong to another, to him who has been raised from the dead, in order that we may bear fruit for God. For while we were living in the flesh, our sinful passions, aroused by the law, were at work in our members to bear fruit for death. (Romans 7:4-5)

And let our people learn to devote themselves to good works, so as to help cases of urgent need, and not be unfruitful. (Titus 3:14)

But the fruit of the Spirit is love, joy, peace, patience, kindness, goodness, faithfulness, gentleness, self-control; against such things there is no law. (Galatians 5:22-23)

But the wisdom from above is first pure, then peaceable, gentle, open to reason, full of mercy and good fruits, impartial and sincere. (James 3:17)

As for that in the good soil, they are those who, hearing the word, hold it fast in an honest and good heart, and bear fruit with patience. (Luke 8:15)

So as to walk in a manner worthy of the Lord, fully pleasing to him: bearing fruit in every good work and increasing in the knowledge of God. (Colossians 1:10)

The Prophet Isaiah told us that there will be no end to the increase of God's kingdom (Isaiah 9:7). We need to look inward and evaluate what aspects of the kingdom are increasing in our lives. Kingdom people are called to bear fruit and have the knowledge of God increasing in their lives.

Chapter 3
What Does *Fulfilled* Mean?

When we declare that Jesus is the fulfillment of everything the Prophets spoke about, what exactly does that mean? Does *fulfilled* mean everything ceased after Jesus ascended to heaven? Did the kingdom stop increasing? Here are some definitions by dictionary.com.

Fulfilled means "to satisfy (requirements, obligations, etc.), to bring to an end; finish or complete, to develop the full potential of" (Dictionary.Com).

There were many promises of a coming Messiah in the Old Testament, which were fulfilled by Jesus alone. They were fulfilled in a single event and will never be repeated.

1. Messiah would be born in Bethlehem: Micah 5:2
2. Messiah would be born from a virgin: Isaiah 7:14
3. Messiah would be from the tribe of Judah: Genesis 49:10
4. Messiah would be the heir to the throne of King David: 2 Samuel 7:12-13
5. Messiah would be called Immanuel: Isaiah 7:4
6. Messiah would spend time in Egypt: Jeremiah 31:15
7. Messiah would be preceded by a messenger: Isaiah 40:35
8. Messiah would be rejected by his own people: Psalms 69:8
9. Messiah would be a Nazarene: Isaiah 11:1
10. Messiah would be crucified with criminals: Isaiah 53:12
11. Messiah would be mocked and ridiculed: Psalms 22:7-8
12. Messiah would not have his bones broken: Exodus 12:46, Psalms 34:20
13. Messiah would have his side pierced by soldiers: Zechariah 12:10
14. Messiah would be raised from the dead: Psalms 24:7-10
15. Messiah would be seated at God's right hand: Psalms 110:1
16. Messiah would make a sacrifice for sin: Isaiah 53:5-12

17. Messiah would be king of an everlasting kingdom: 2 Samuel 7:13
18. Messiah would possess a special anointing of the Holy Spirit: Psalms 45:7

The Old Testament is filled with many such prophetic words about the Messiah. These prophecies were 'fulfilled in a single event.' While we have so many that were fulfilled completely in the ministry of Christ while he was on earth, it might seem reasonable to conclude that all Messianic prophecies work in the same way. I believe this would be a grave error. When we read words from the Prophets which have direct correlation to an event in the life of Jesus, it is important to look deeper at the passage. Does *fulfilled* mean that the promises and the conditions of the Abrahamic, Davidic and the New Covenant have no meaning for the church? What about the numerous Old Testament passages about the kingdom?

The prophetic words in the Old Testament do not stop having a meaning after Jesus left the earth. Here is a sample of prophetic words, which were not limited to Jesus in his life events but continued to be worked out in the church. In section II these and others will be examined more closely.

1. **Isaiah 9:6-7** The kingdom of the Messiah will always be increasing. Since the kingdom began in the first century, we cannot limit its fulfillment to that time frame, but look to how this promise is being fulfilled through the church in the present and for all ages to come.
2. **Psalms 68:18** The Messiah gives gifts to men. These are the five-fold ministry gifts to the church. These gifts were given from the Ascended Christ. The time of Christ was their beginning, not their end.
3. **Psalms 80:17** The Messiah is God's man at his right hand. This is his place of authority over his kingdom, which continues to be manifested in the church.

4. **Daniel 7:13-14** The dominion of the Messiah was foretold to be everlasting. The kingdom began in the first century, in the hearts of believers and it continues in his people today.

5. **Jeremiah 31:31** The Messiah established a new covenant: This new covenant is the church's continuous agreement with God. It did not end with the person of Jesus in the first century but continues in his body - the church.

6. **Isaiah 49:7** The salvation of the Messiah will go to the ends of the earth. Even though the message of the kingdom went to the known world in the first century (Matthew 24:14) as a witness, the 'discipling of nations' is ongoing; it is fulfilled by the work of the church.

7. **Jeremiah 33:17** David shall never lack a man to sit on his throne. Jesus fulfills the promise and is the new David. His reign on the throne is everlasting. This is not a single event fulfillment, but one that has a beginning and then the results flow out to all generations.

8. **Psalms 22:27** All the families of the earth will worship the Messiah. This is a promise to past, present and future nations. A ministry of the church is to fill the nations with worship.

9. **Psalms 22:28** The Messiah will rule over the nations. Again, this is not limited to first-century nations.

10. **Isaiah 49:6** The Messiah will be the light to the Gentiles. The inclusion of Gentiles in the church did not take place until 20 years after the cross. This was not fulfilled in the life-time of Jesus but was the result of his death and resurrection. Sharing the light of the Messiah is being fulfilled in the church.

11. **Isaiah 54:1-3** The children of the Gentiles will be greater in number than the children of old covenant Israel. Their offspring will possess the nations. This prophecy is being fulfilled now and will continue to be fulfilled in the future.

12. **Isaiah 65:18-19** Jerusalem was created for joy and God will *be glad in my people.*" This is not fulfilled by old

covenant Israel. The 'people of God' are those who are 'in Christ.'

13. **Isaiah 59:21** The result of the new covenant will be the presence of the Holy Spirit and the words of God, which will not depart out of his people's mouths, nor from their children's offspring, forever. This is a clear word of prophecy found in the Old Testament, that is being fulfilled in the church.

14. **Daniel 7:18** The saints of the most high - which is now the church - will receive and possess the kingdom *"forever, forever and ever."*

15. **Amos 9:11** The tabernacle of David will be rebuilt. This is not a prophecy for a third temple. God has one true temple, which is his people - the church.

16. **Habakkuk 2:14** The earth will be filled with the knowledge of the glory of the Lord. This verse is a key promise for the continued advancement of the kingdom on earth.

17. **Zechariah 6:12** The branch (prophecy about the Messiah) shall build the temple. Through the death and resurrection of Jesus, the church was established and is being built in every generation. The church, not a physical building, is the temple Jesus is building.

18. **Joel 2:28** In the last days God will pour out his Spirit. This was fulfilled on the Day of Pentecost and remains a promise to all those not even born. The pouring out of the Spirit is a promise for all generations. This is clearly being fulfilled in the church. It was more than a single event, it continues today. Everyday there are people around the world who are beneficiaries of what Joel prophesied.

If we remove these and a plethora of other promises of the kingdom, we are left with only a handful of New Testament verses to inform us of the extent of the kingdom on earth. My conviction is that many Old Testament prophecies remain unfulfilled. They were *fulfilled* in the sense of being made possible through Christ. They are being fulfilled in the church today and they have a future fulfillment in the coming generations. What we see today is not all we will see. The kingdom is growing. The kingdom is advancing. The kingdom will be filled with praise and righteousness. We are at the beginning. We have seen great advances of the kingdom since the Day of Pentecost and the church will see even greater advancements in the coming generations. We need to read the Old Testament with a view from the New Testament. This was the "Apostolic Hermeneutic" used by the first followers of Jesus. They read the Old Testament, considering the radical changes brought about by their Messiah - Jesus.

Since the core message of this book is finding the 'Rich Root' of the Old Testament promises, we will return to these and other passages in the second section. First we need to visit the importance of 'hermeneutics' in the interpretation of Old Testament promises and prophecies.

Chapter 4
The Old Testament through the Eyes of Jesus and the Apostles

We have set out to show how the "rich root" of Israel represents the covenants and kingdom promises from the prophets. The covenants are limited to two; Abrahamic and Davidic, and the kingdom promises are found in most of the prophetic books. If the Old Testament covenants and promises are completely fulfilled and are now obsolete, we should expect them to have received little attention from Jesus and his apostles. Yet, this is not the case. How did Jesus and the apostles read the Old Testament? Was it the inspired Word of God? Did they see it as an authoritative source for what was being accomplished in their time? We will begin with Jesus and what he said about Abraham.

How did Jesus view Abraham? How did the Jews of the first-century see Abraham? And the key question, how did Jesus see himself in relationship to Abraham? These are crucial themes in the New Testament. Once we can recognize the Abraham question in the gospels, what did the Apostles teach concerning the church and Abraham? Since the church is added to the 'rich root' of Israel and Abraham is a central figure in the story of Israel, we need to dive into the teachings of Paul, since he wrote the most about Abraham.

Before we examine Jesus and the apostles, let's look at a passage in Matthew's gospel about how John the Baptist used Abraham in his tirade against the Jewish leaders.

Now John wore a garment of camel's hair and a leather belt around his waist, and his food was locusts and wild honey. Then Jerusalem and all Judea and all the region about the Jordan were going out to him, and they were baptized by him in the river Jordan, confessing their sins.

But when he saw many of the Pharisees and Sadducees coming to his baptism, he said to them, "You brood of vipers! Who warned you to flee from the wrath to come? Bear fruit in keeping with repentance. And do not presume to say to yourselves, 'We have Abraham as our father,' for I tell you, God is able from these stones to raise up children for Abraham. Even now the axe is laid to the root of the trees. Every tree therefore that does not bear good fruit is cut down and thrown into the fire. (Matthew 3:4-10)

Matthew writes about how John came into conflict with many of the Pharisees and Sadducees who came to him for baptism. Every time I read this passage, I wonder why the Pharisees would come to him in the first place. Were they ready to repent? Not according to John. Their actions were hypocritical, and their hearts were exposed. The river scene sets up a New Testament pattern, one in which those Jewish leaders and their followers were headed straight towards judgment.

John the Baptist did not wait for the religious leaders to claim their allegiance to Abraham. He knew their hearts and knew their intentions were filled with deceit. They lacked any sincere repentance. I wish we had more of that specific dialogue, but what Matthew does describe is a precursor of the type of debates Jesus would have later. John the Baptist knew the central argument of these religious leaders would be their connection to Abraham. They were the chosen people of God and compared to all the other nations - God's favorite. John calls them, "*A brood of vipers*" and if we think about it, Jesus did the same (Matthew 23:33).

Abraham and David are the two men of the Old Testament that are given significant space in the New Testament. If we look at the whole Bible, it is remarkable how many times they are mentioned. Depending on which Bible version we use and how the proper names are listed we can figure out the number of times Abraham, David and Jesus are mentioned in the Bible.

Abraham - 312

David - 1141

Jesus - 1254

Whatever we think of these numbers, one thing is certain, all three are central to the story of the Bible. The story of all three comes together in the opening sentence of the New Testament.

The book of the genealogy of Jesus Christ, the son of David, the son of Abraham. (Matthew 1:1)

Our reading of the New Testament begins with the gospel of Matthew. His first sentence builds a theological structure for the rest of the New Testament. Jesus is a son. Son of Abraham. Son of David. These must be kept in harmony with each other. Teaching Jesus is the Son of God and neglecting Abraham will lead to misunderstanding the covenantal dimensions of the gospel. If we abandon David, we end up with a gospel without the kingdom. Jesus being the son of Abraham and the son of David must be kept in proper tension to forge out our theology of the New Testament. It is at the heart of our gospel.

I tell you, many will come from east and west and recline at table with Abraham, Isaac, and Jacob in the kingdom of heaven (Matthew 8:11)

During this conversation about the healing of the Centurion's servant, Jesus brings up an eschatological scenario. The typical dispensational interpretation is that this dinner takes place between the rapture and the second coming of Christ. Of course, in heaven. The people in the first century never thought *"the kingdom of Heaven"* was a code word for heaven. This statement by Jesus was not about dying and going to heaven. The kingdom of God or Matthew's version - the kingdom of heaven, is the hope for this world. God's kingdom comes from heaven but is for the earth. The main point that Jesus is making is one of great expansion of his kingdom. Many will come to the table and be joined to the God of Abraham, Isaac and Jacob. This is happening now! God's plans are far greater than the renewal of only Israel. The Centurion is a first-fruits of the multitudes of Gentiles, which shall come into the kingdom of God. Gentiles and Jews sitting together, eating and enjoying the goodness of God's kingdom would have been an image most Jews of the day would have found disturbing to say the least.

We notice that we are not sitting at the table - we, "Recline." Reclining around a mat or table was a common Roman/Greek tradition. Life was not so ordered and hectic as today. Everything moved more slowly, and eating was a social event, a time for fellowship and sharing. Even today, taking the evening meal in many cultures is more than eating. When my wife and I first went to Bulgaria, this custom of having 'lengthy evening meals' was one of the many culture shocks. If the meal began around 9:00 PM, it would conclude around midnight. This was the way of life in the first-century for Jesus and the disciples. They did not consider 'laying around a table' as the 'waste of time' many would consider it today.

What we have in this kingdom saying is that there will be many people coming into the fellowship of God's family. We are all connected to Abraham through Christ.

Charles J. Ellicott (1819-1905), an English theologian, puts these words in proper perspective: "Many shall come from the east and the west. It is clear that our Lord saw in the centurion the first-fruits of the wide harvest of the future. Like the words of the Baptist in Matthew 3:9, what He now said contained, by implication, the whole gospel, which St. Paul preached to the Gentiles. "East and west," even without the formal addition of "north and south," which we find in the parallel passage of Luke 13:29, were used as limits that included all the nations of the earth."[9]

Jesus connects Abraham with the expansion of the gospel to the people of all nations. He is not the exclusive patriarch of the Jews.

---

[9] Charles, J. Ellicott, Ellicott's Bible Commentary for English Readers Volume 1, Kindle Edition, Delmarva Publications, 2015

Your father Abraham rejoiced that he would see my day. He saw it and was glad." So the Jews said to him, "You are not yet fifty years old, and have you seen Abraham?" Jesus said to them, "Truly, truly, I say to you, before Abraham was, I am." So they picked up stones to throw at him, but Jesus hid himself and went out of the temple. (John 8:56-59)

John Gill wrote about how Abraham and all the prophets looked forward to the day on which Israel's Messiah would come to earth.

"Your father Abraham rejoiced to see my day, or "he was desirous to see my day", as the Syriac and Arabic versions rightly render the word; or "very desirous", as the Persic version: and indeed, this was what many kings, prophets and righteous men were desirous of, even of seeing the Messiah and his day: we often read of, "the days of the Messiah"[10]

Gill states it well, that the whole of Old Testament is filled with righteous people, eagerly anticipating the coming of Yahweh's Christ. We cannot understand the meaning of Jesus and his kingdom apart from what was foreseen in the Old Testament.

The fact that Abraham looked ahead and saw the Messiah was not what the religious leaders were angered by. When Jesus said, *"Before Abraham, I AM"*, the wrath of the people was stirred to the point of murder. They wanted to kill him right there. Why? Without a doubt, Jesus was claiming his divinity here. The Bible commentary by Jamieson, Fausset and Brown makes this point, when it says Jesus, "Existed before Abraham had a being; in other words, existed before creation, or eternally (as John 1:1). The Jews understood Him, since "*then took they up stones to cast at Him,*" just as they had done before, when they saw that He made Himself equal with God (John 5:18)".[11]

---

[10] John Gill, Gill's Commentary and Exposition of the Old and New Testaments, Baker Book House, 1980

[11] Robert Jamieson, A. R. Fausset, David Brown, Jamieson, Fausset, and Brown's Commentary On the Whole Bible Hardcover, OSNOVA; 2 edition, 2011

The Apostles and Abraham

Know then that it is those of faith who are the sons of Abraham. And the Scripture, foreseeing that God would justify the Gentiles by faith, preached the gospel beforehand to Abraham, saying, "In you shall all the nations be blessed." So then, those who are of faith are blessed along with Abraham, the man of faith. (Galatians 3:7-8)

Apostle Paul, being the key architect of New Testament theology, had plenty to say about Abraham. Commenting on everything he wrote about Abraham would be a book in itself. Nevertheless, what we have here in a few words comes close to encapsulating his Abrahamic teaching. Paul did not avoid the central issue of Israel, the church and Abraham. Abraham is the key to unraveling the connection between Israel and the church. Therefore, Paul unleashes a full and often contentious treatment of the subject.

He begins by stating what the Jews had to hear and hear clearly; that with the coming of Jesus the only way to continue being a 'son of Abraham' was by faith; it was no longer by nationality or through the Mosaic covenant.

I find the wording of Paul, that the "Scripture" preached the gospel a little odd, but full of revelation. Normally we would say, "Abraham preached the Scriptures", but that is not how Paul wrote it. What is said here is the Old Testament's version of the "Gospel of the Kingdom."

Chapter 5
A Christocentric Hermeneutic

This and the following chapter will briefly outline two methods of reading the Prophets. I see them as building towards the same purpose and not in a hermeneutical competition. The first is called "A Christocentric Hermeneutic" and the Second - "A Theological Interpretation of Scripture (TIS)." Both tend to be academic in their presentation, especially TIS, so the challenge here is to bring out what is needed and useful for digging deeper in the 'rich root' of the Old Testament. Doing so will enhance not only our understanding of the kingdom, but also our spiritual growth.

It's very interesting to read how the authors of the New Testament use passages from the Old Testament. They do not seem overly concerned to find out what the original author had in mind, nor the historical context. The truth of their hermeneutic would not pass as legitimate by current church authorities.

Richard Bauckham, retired professor of New Testament Studies at the University of St Andrews, Scotland, makes a fascinating statement about New Testament scholars' uneasiness to seriously examine how the First-century Apostles interpreted the Old Testament prophets.

"The fulfilment proves both that the prophecies were inspired by God and that Jesus was the Messiah that God himself sent. This kind of apologetic appeal to messianic prophecy is less often heard today. I think this must be at least partly due to the influence of biblical scholars, who have insisted on a historicizing kind of exegesis, that tries to read the prophecies as they would have been heard at the time they were written and very often find that this differs considerably from the way the writers of the New Testament read them, when they interpreted them as referring to Jesus. I sense that New Testament scholars are sometimes a little embarrassed by the gap that seems to open between the historical meaning of the Old

Testament texts and the way they were read by New Testament Christians."[12]

It is this 'gap' that must lead us in our exploration of not only how the Apostles read the Hebrew prophets, but also helps us determine the method they used. At this point, it is time to introduce a hermeneutic that will help immensely in closing this gap when reading the Old Testament Prophets. It is the Christocentric method.

Christocentric Hermeneutic

How does the Christocentric method assist in properly interpreting the Hebrew Prophets? How is this method different than 'traditional hermeneutics' and what advantage does it provide?

We begin by seeing the Old Testament through the lens of the finished work of Christ, we can apply the 'spiritual realities' that came with the new covenant.

After studying various books on 'Christocentric' interpretation, I realized I had been using this basic method for years. Viewing the ongoing work of the church through the words of the Prophets was not new to me, because I see the church as the new covenant version of ancient Israel. I knew that the Prophets spoke of the Messiah's kingdom and that the church is the only people of the kingdom. Therefore, seeing the ongoing work of the church through the words of the Prophets was not new to me. What I have come to understand through my recent studies is how I can build a 'checklist' of Christocentric principles.

Australian theologian Graeme Goldsworthy: "The hermeneutical question about the whole Bible correlates with the question, 'What do you think of Christ?' ... The hermeneutical center of the Bible is therefore Jesus in his being and in his saving acts – the Jesus of the gospel. ... We can say that, while not all Scripture is the gospel, all

---

[12] Richard Bauckham, Macbride Sermon on the application of Messianic Prophecy, Oxford University, 2003, http://www.richardbauckham.co.uk/ uploads/Sermons/ Messianic%20Prophecy.pdf

Scripture is related to the gospel that is its center. ... The Bible makes a very radical idea inescapable: not only is the gospel the interpretive norm for the whole Bible, but there is an important sense in which Jesus Christ is the mediator of the meaning of everything that exists. In other words, *the gospel is the hermeneutical norm for the whole of reality*".[13]

Goldsworthy says the gospel is the interpretive norm for the whole Bible. I agree. Yet, I think the 'Gospel' must be defined to be able to gain the most insight into how a Christocentric hermeneutic works. For me the 'Gospel' is the good news of the Messiah and his kingdom. If we limit the term to the 'cross', we lose sight of the kingdom. The cross of Jesus was necessary to bring us into the kingdom. For God's people to enter his kingdom, a radical reordering of creation was needed. Sin, death and Satan needed to be defeated. Sin needed to be forgiven. The Holy Spirt needed to come and dwell in the new 'eschatological' people of God (the Israel of God). The dramatic changes which were brought about by the death and resurrection of Jesus can be summarized by what Paul said in the book of Colossians.

He has delivered us from the domain of darkness and transferred us to the kingdom of his beloved Son, in whom we have redemption, the forgiveness of sins. (Colossians 1:13-14)

Our beginning point in a Christocentric method of interpretation is that we start our exegesis through the revelation of Jesus and his kingdom, as recorded in the New Testament. We must not disregard the reason for Jesus' coming to earth - to announce and bring in the kingdom of God.

Another term closely related to *Christocentric* is an *Apostolic Hermeneutic.*

---

[13] Graeme Goldsworthy, Gospel-Centered Hermeneutics, https://www.monergism .com/topics/hermeneutics/christocentric-hermeneutics

R. Scott Clark wrote an article called, "Was There an Apostolic Hermeneutic and Can We Imitate It?" In a humorous and potent fashion Clark shows how the dispensational hermeneutic does not work.

"Yes, and yes. No, it's not in the Scofield Reference or Ryrie Study Bibles... It isn't that complicated. Pay close attention here: *The Apostolic hermeneutic is to see Christ at the center of all of Scripture.* We're not reading him *into* Scripture. We're refusing to read him out of it. There, I said it. That's what it is. Perhaps the reason our dispensational friends cannot see it is because they are blinded by their rationalism. They know *a priori* what the organizing principle of Scripture *must* be, and it isn't God the Son, it's national Israel. "What my net can't catch must not be butterflies." Do they ever stop to think that the trouble could be their net? Does it ever trouble them that any system leading to the conclusion that one day the Lamb of God, who takes away the sin of the world (John 1:29, 36), who is presently ruling the nations (Acts 2:36; Rev 5:12-13) is going to sit on a throne in Jerusalem to watch sinful human priests slaughter lambs?"[14]

Clark continues to discuss his dispensational criticism that a Christocentric hermeneutic is a 'spiritual' rather than a 'literal' method of reading the Bible.

"A Platonizing dualism that sets the material against the physical. This same tendency produces a similar hermeneutic among many American dispensationalists as well. This dualistic tendency explains why dispensationalists refer to the apostolic hermeneutic as "spiritualizing." Yes, it does, but not in the way they think. "Spiritual" in Paul's vocabulary does not mean "immaterial", but "of the Holy Spirit." The same Spirit who inspired Moses also inspired Paul. There is a "Spiritual" interpretation of Holy Scripture

---

[14] R. Scott Clark, https://heidelblog.net/2008/09/was-there-an-apostolic-hermeneutic-and-can-we-imitate-it/

that focuses on the God-Man who entered history and around whom all of God's self-revelation is organized."[15]

If we remain committed to only reading the Prophets in the same manner that their contemporaries would have understood them, we miss out on the Apostolic revelation that comes through a radical change, that was brought about by the new covenant.

Richard Bauckham: "When we read the Old Testament that way, I think we can see that a purely historicizing exegesis of messianic prophecies is not in fact adequate to their nature. They belong to the dynamic movement of the Old Testament towards the future. They are key expressions of that movement. We miss their real significance if we try to tie them down to the circumstances of their original composition. They are open texts, which meaning is not complete until the promises they make finally find fulfilment in reality.[16]"

I fully agree with Bauckham that these Old Testament prophecies are 'dynamic' in nature and unless we unlock the new covenant revelation within them, we "miss their real significance." By stripping away the voice of the Prophets, we are losing many passages, which describe the kingdom.

Christ the Full Revelation of God

The primarily reason for viewing the whole of Scripture through the lens of Christ is because he is the full revelation of God. We see this in the New Testament.

1. Jesus is the purest, the most complete, and the highest revelation of who God is.

---

[15] Ibid.

[16] Richard Bauckham, Macbride Sermon on the application of Messianic Prophecy, Oxford University, 2003, http://www.richardbauckham.co.uk/uploads/Sermons/Messianic%20Prophecy.pdf

2. The God of the Old Testament must be seen through the lens of Jesus, hence, Christocentric.

3. Jesus is the final expression of God and therefore He is the authoritative standard to interpret all Scripture, including the Old Testament.

4. To understand the whole of Scripture, it is imperative we have a 'New Covenant' revelation. Therefore, we read from a "Theological Interpretation' based on the new covenant.

New Testament Scripture Affirming the Centrality of Christ

All things have been handed over to me by my Father, and no one knows the Son except the Father, and no one knows the Father except the Son and anyone to whom the Son chooses to reveal him. (Matthew 11:27)

When we view Jesus as the one and only person to fully know the Father, it opens a method of interpreting Scripture. The hope we have is that by being "in Christ", we will also grow to know the Father as the Son does. Since the Son reveals the Father, we must pay attention to what Jesus teaches and what the Apostles say about him. The importance of this is because if any portion of Scripture 'seems' to offer a different view than that of Jesus, we had better take a fresh look and examine our basic principles of interpretation.

And beginning with Moses and all the Prophets, he interpreted to them in all the Scriptures the things concerning himself. (Luke 24:27)

I am the way, and the truth, and the life. (John 14:6)

That their hearts may be encouraged, being knit together in love, to reach all the riches of full assurance of understanding and the knowledge of God's mystery, which is Christ, in whom are hidden all the treasures of wisdom and knowledge. (Colossians 2:2-3)

He is the image of the invisible God, the firstborn of all creation.
For by him all things were created, in heaven and on earth, visible
and invisible, whether thrones or dominions or rulers or
authorities—all things were created through him and for him. And
he is before all things, and in him all things hold together. And he is
the head of the body, the church. He is the beginning, the firstborn
from the dead, that in everything he might be preeminent. For in him
all the fullness of God was pleased to dwell, and through him to
reconcile to himself all things, whether on earth or in heaven,
making peace by the blood of his cross. (Colossians 1:15-20)

In my Bible study book, *Kingdom First*, I quoted Pastor and
theologian Greg Boyd. He is one of the foremost theologians in this
area, therefore I will quote him here also.

Greg Boyd: "These earliest disciples assumed, as did the church
tradition that followed them, that Jesus was "the goal and fulfillment
of the whole Old Testament" and therefore, "the interpretive key to
the Bible."[17]

Jesus is the key. Any hermeneutic to understanding the Bible must
recognize that Jesus the Christ is the "interpretive key."

Boyd continues: "The authors of the NT were not interested in
discerning the original meaning of passages to place alongside of
the revelation of God in Christ; they were rather intent on
discerning the meaning passages had when read in the light of
Christ. This "new" and "creative" approach was adopted by NT
authors because in the words of Moule, "Christ was found to be
more authoritative than scripture…in the sense of fulfilling and
transcending it, not abolishing it."[18]

---

[17] Greg Boyd, Crucifixion of the Warrior God, Fortress Press, Minneapolis, page
95
[18] Greg Boyd, Crucifixion of the Warrior God, Fortress Press, Minneapolis, page
98

As we go forward with a Christocentric hermeneutic, it may be worthwhile to address what our interpretation 'cannot' mean, when applied to the Old Testament Prophets.

1. The interpretation cannot negate the coming of Christ and his establishment of the kingdom of God in the First century.

2. The interpretation cannot be applied to an Israel that does not exist. (This applies to Old Testament Israel which was the covenant nation until the New Covenant replaced it)

3. The interpretation cannot violate any doctrine taught by the New Testament Apostles.

When the old covenant became obsolete (Hebrews 8:13) old Israel ceased as a covenant nation and those Jews that 'believed' entered the "*one new man*" (Ephesians 2:14-15) of the new covenant. We have a political nation today, called Israel, and we need to pray for their conversion to Christ, so they can enjoy the blessings of the kingdom.

Using Jesus as the highest authority for interpreting Scripture does not violate the authors' original meaning, but it acknowledges that these men were moved by the Holy Spirit when they wrote. Once the time arrives and certain events occur, then, we can see the 'prophetic element' that was there all the time.

Closely associated to the *Christocentric method* is one called *Theological Interpretation of Scripture*. It is this 'theological' method we will turn to now.

Chapter 6
Theological Interpretation

A hermeneutic called *The Theological Interpretation of Scripture* (TIS) helps us understand the Old Testament in view of New Testament theology. TIS is a growing and complex hermeneutic. In my opinion, it needs more clarification as a hermeneutical system. Here is a beginning definition.

Theological interpretation of Scripture can be defined as "those readings of biblical texts, that consciously seek to do justice to the perceived theological nature of the texts and embrace the influence of theology (corporate and personal; past and present) upon the interpreter's enquiry, context, and method."[19]

Although short, this definition provides several key points. First, it points out that there are certain texts, that seem to jump out and point to the need for a 'theological nature' of what is being said. It is more than a historical statement of fact. This is especially true in those prophetic passages in the Old Testament, which point to the coming of Jesus and his Messianic reign. Second, we learn that the serious interpreter can look to the future (from when it was written) for greater understanding. This is helpful. I believe we understand more of Isaiah's prophecy after the coming of Jesus and the establishment of his kingdom, than we would have before.

Here is another definition, which is more detailed.

"The aim of Theological Interpretation is to read the Bible *as Scripture*, that is, as somehow God's transformative address to the Church here in the present. We may contrast this with the past two centuries of biblical scholarship, whose interests have been primarily *historical*: that is, they were aimed at reconstructing the

---

[19] D. Christopher Spinks, The Bible and the Crisis of Meaning: Debates on the Theological Interpretation of Scripture (T&T Clark, 2007), p. 7.

life, religion, and history of ancient Israel and early Christianity. Here the Biblical writings are treated as ancient artefacts, which provide windows into the past, where they are firmly located, the differences between the ancient world and the contemporary world being stressed. The model interpreter is the detached and objective *historian*, uninfluenced by theological interests or doctrinal traditions, that may distort or bias interpretation. In contrast, while recognizing the 'historical' character of the Bible, Theological Interpretation will not relegate it to the past, nor will it separate theology from interpretation. Grounded in the theological continuity between God's people in all ages, the Bible is read as the 'word of God' *to us*."[20]

One point stands out in this definition. We cannot separate theology from interpretation. We cannot understand Old Testament texts without applying first the theology of the New Testament. Yes, some texts are historical, and those should not be stretched or allegorized beyond their plain meaning. Nevertheless, there are many Old Testament passages where more is needed. The mystery of the 'Christ Event' must be viewed before arriving at a proper and valuable understanding.

With these definitions in mind, I will simply define 'Theological Interpretation' as applying the theology of the present kingdom/new covenant and then viewing the Old Testament promises through them. When we read a passage in the Old Testament that seems Messianic (A prophecy about the coming of Jesus and his reign), how should we proceed with the interpretation? A theological interpretation means we interpret the Old Testament from our New Testament theology. Therefore, it is necessary to form convictions of the New Testament before we begin applying them to Old Testament passages.

If our view of the kingdom of God is one of a future 1,000-year reign, based upon a literal reading of the number 1,000 in Revelation

---

[20] Edmund Fearon, Theological Interpretation, Hermeneutica, https:// hermeneutica.wordpress.com/essays/what-is-theological-interpretation/

20, our reading of Old Testament passages about the kingdom will follow suit. On the opposing side, if our view of the kingdom is one of a first-century establishment, and we interpret the 1,000 years in Revelation 20 as symbolic, our readings of the Prophets will be much different. We often use a theological hermeneutic without realizing it.

Throughout the Old Testament and especially the Prophets, there are passages, which shed light on the new covenant church. This is my conviction and therefore we need to grasp some basic foundational truths from the New Testament, whereby we can begin to apply both a *Christocentric hermeneutic* and a *Theological Interpretation*.

One example of how TIS should be applied is found in the creation account (Genesis 1:1). Genesis is a straightforward account of creation, *"In the beginning, God created the heavens and the earth."* As the history of Israel develops, this is all they needed to know about creation. It was their God, the God of Israel, who was the creator of heaven and earth. Therefore, they worshipped the one and true God, whereby all nations had to obey and worship. This worked well, until the Apostles of the New Testament went back and retold the creation account, considering their revelation of Christ.

All things were made through him, and without him was not anything made that was made. (John 1:3)

He was in the world, and the world was made through him, yet the world did not know him. (John 1:10)

He is the image of the invisible God, the firstborn of all creation. For by him all things were created, in heaven and on earth, visible and invisible, whether thrones or dominions or rulers or authorities —all things were created through him and for him. (Colossians 1:15-16)

Yet for us there is one God, the Father, from whom are all things and for whom we exist, and one Lord, Jesus Christ, through whom are all things and through whom we exist. (I Corinthians 8:6)

Christians today can read these verses and pass them by, without recognizing the radical and revolutionary nature of what the early followers of Jesus wrote. For any first-century Jew, these words were blasphemy. To claim that another being, and a human at that, was with God and part of the creation process, was unbelievable. Yet, this was the bold claim of the Apostles.

Jews were expecting their Messiah, yet, for them he was to be a man, a king type person like David not a person claiming higher status than Abraham. Here we have both a Christocentric way of reading the Old Testament and the usage of a theological approach. To say that Christ was the person involved in the creation of all things and then to say all things were created for him, this was a theological understanding of who Christ was. He was God's eternal son, who was with God and was part of God.

By using these methods, we come to understand more fully Genesis 1:1. Without reading the words of the New Testament back into the first account, we learn only part of the story. Now the story is complete.

Whenever the Apostles had the opportunity to reveal that Jesus was the Christ and part of God, they did so. They took the creation story from Genesis and added in what was missing - the role of the Son in the creation account.

Let's look at another example, a more difficult one, to see how we should interpret it.

We usually think all Psalms were written in the time of King David, which is around 1,000 B.C., yet, according to the Septuagint version, there is a psalm (Ps. 137:1) that is from Jeremiah. The Septuagint includes an explanation, "For David. By Jeremias, in the Captivity."[21]

---

[21] translated from the Greek Septuagint by the Holy Transfiguration Monastery. (1974). The Psalter According to the Seventy. 1987, second printing. Boston MA: Holy Transfiguration Monastery. p. 241.

By the waters of Babylon, there we sat down and wept, when we remembered Zion. (Psalms 137:1)

The children of Israel were captives in Babylon and dreaming of Jerusalem. At the end of this prayer there is a note of praise for their God, the God of Israel, who would replay the captors with judgment.

O daughter of Babylon, doomed to be destroyed, blessed shall he be who repays you with what you have done to us! Blessed shall he be who takes your little ones and dashes them against the rock! (Psalms 137:8-9)

As horrible as these words seem to us, within their time and history this would have been accepted as a normal response to Israel's enemies. They wanted their God to move forcibly against their enemies and destroy them in the most brutal fashion.

Today, if our pastor stood and prayed such things, the whole church would be in shock. Yet, I have heard things spoken in churches against our perceived enemies, that would almost equal this. How should we read it? First, we cannot deny the historic words. They were written and are now a part of the Holy Scriptures. Their meaning is not shrouded in mystery; it is clear. God's people desired the babies of their enemies to be dashed upon the rocks and killed.

Applying a theological understanding to this and other passages is necessary, so we know how to think about and how to pray for our enemies. Should we be praying these types of prayers against our enemies? What did Jesus teach?

Jesus taught we are to love our enemies, not kill them. Do we see a change of God's nature in Jesus? Reading the Old Testament, it seems like God was responsible for ethnic cleansing, genocide, and the murder of babies. This is disturbing. Was Jesus the true expression of God within history, or was there a change in God's nature with the incarnation? Since we believe the nature of God does not change, we must look to the life and teachings of Jesus.

First, we must review what Jesus taught about treating our enemies.

To the contrary, "*if your enemy is hungry, feed him; if he is thirsty, give him something to drink; for by so doing you will heap burning coals on his head.*" Do not be overcome by evil but overcome evil with good. (Romans 12:20-21)

"*But I say to you who hear, Love your enemies, do good to those who hate you, bless those who curse you, pray for those who abuse you.* (Luke 6:27-28)

"*You have heard that it was said, 'An eye for an eye and a tooth for a tooth.' But I say to you, Do not resist the one who is evil. But if anyone slaps you on the right cheek, turn to him the other also.* (Matthew 5:38-39)

You have heard that it was said, 'You shall love your neighbor and hate your enemy.' But I say to you, Love your enemies and pray for those who persecute you, so that you may be sons of your Father who is in heaven. For he makes his sun rise on the evil and on the good, and sends rain on the just and on the unjust. (Matthew 5:43-45)

So whatever you wish that others would do to you, do also to them, for this is the Law and the Prophets. (Matthew 7:12)

Here is a simple, rule-of-thumb guide for behavior: Ask yourself what you want people to do for you, then grab the initiative and do it for them. Add up God's Law and Prophets and this is what you get. (Matthew 7:12 The Message)

This is interesting. Jesus taught his disciples to act toward others in the same manner they would want to be treated. Then he says something extraordinary. He states that by living in this manner, we are acting in accordance with all the "Law and the Prophets." Jesus said this is the essence of what is taught in the Old Testament. Therefore, we must come to agree with Jesus, that our understanding of the many passages, where God is portrayed as a violent deity, may need to be adjusted. As Theologian Greg Boyd often says, "Something else is going on here."

Then Jesus said to him, "Put your sword back into its place. For all who take the sword will perish by the sword. Do you think that I cannot appeal to my Father, and he will at once send me more than twelve legions of angels? But how then should the Scriptures be fulfilled, that it must be so?" (Matthew 26:52-54)

Do not repay evil with evil or insult with insult, but with blessing, because to this you were called so that you may inherit a blessing. (I Peter 3:9)

Teacher, which is the great commandment in the Law?" And he said to him, "You shall love the Lord your God with all your heart and with all your soul and with all your mind. This is the great and first commandment. And a second is like it: You shall love your neighbor as yourself. On these two commandments depend all the Law and the Prophets." (Matthew 22:36-40)

Theological Changes in the New Testament

New Testament Foundations Needed to Interpret the Old Testament

Jesus came as Israel's Messiah.

As a nation they rejected the Messiah. They were the branches, that were broken off in Romans 11.

The believing remnant of First-century Jews came into the new covenant and 'replaced' the old covenant people. If there is any 'replacement' going on, it was 'Jews replacing Jews,' as God's people. It was several decades before Gentiles became part of the olive tree.

The death of Jesus took a few years to be fully understood.

Israel misunderstood the nature of the kingdom, even though there was a good amount of Old Testament passages to give them a better perspective.

Entering God's kingdom was by spiritual transformation and therefore sin, death and Satan had to be defeated.

At the cross Jesus made the forgiveness of sin a possibility and once and for all defeated the realm of darkness.

In the resurrection and enthronement, Jesus was given dominion - a kingdom and glory.

Jesus reigns from the right hand of God, which fulfills the promise to David, that one of his heirs would reign forever.

The church was born on the day of Pentecost.

The Kingdom of God is a reign of grace.

The kingdom of God is righteousness, peace and joy in the Holy Spirit. The kingdom is a walk in the Spirit, not a life of laws.

The Old Covenant ended at the cross and vanished, when the temple in Jerusalem was destroyed in 70 AD. This ended the 'last days' of the old covenant.

The kingdom of God begins with Jesus and will increase throughout the generations, without end. The knowledge of his glory will cover the earth and the church will come into the unity of faith and of the mature status of Christ.

The Physical city of Jerusalem becomes the spiritual New Jerusalem.

The Temple of stone becomes a living temple of God's people.

The sacrifice of animals was replaced by the one-time sacrifice of Jesus on the cross.

Worship is not linked to a location but must be done in Spirit and Truth.

The promise of geographic land to Israel becomes the whole world.

For Apostle Paul, the "Israel of God" (Galatians 6:16) and "the people of the new creation" are the same. The church is the present form of "The Israel of God", created by Jesus, the Messiah.

This is by no means a complete list, but it does provide a starting point to fully understand the 'rich root' found in the prophets of the Old Testament.

There is one additional subject that must be addressed before digging deeper into the Old Testament prophecies. Most likely there will be a cry against a 'Replacement Theology,' since the crux of my position is how the church fulfills the promises originally given to Old Testament Israel. It is the 'elephant' in the room few people like to address.

Christocentric and Theological Interpretation was the Apostles' Hermeneutic

Elements of Christocentric and Theological Interpretation lead us to the Apostolic Interpretation. The New Testament Apostles made considerable changes in how the Old Testament and especially the prophets were to be understood. For them, the coming of Israel's Messiah changed everything!

Here are some beginning guidelines that should be helpful.

1. Everything changed with the arrival of Jesus.

2. No passage can be applied to a covenant that no longer exists.

3. No passage can alter or diminish the character or ministry of Jesus.

4. No passage can eliminate whole groups of people.

5. No passage can be interpreted as 'literal', if it points us to a conclusion different than what the New Testament Apostles wrote.

6. No passage can be eliminated, because it is found in the Old Testament. Correct interpretation is necessary, not dismissal of the passage.

7. The Prophecy of Jeremiah's new covenant has now come to pass through the cross of Jesus. Therefore, all Old

Testament types, shadows, signs, promises and prophecies are fulfilled in Christ and through his body, for the advancement of the kingdom of God on earth.

Chapter 7
Replacement Theology

When there is a discussion about Israel and the church, there is the accusation that we preach a 'Replacement Theology.' Understandably, this comes from dispensationalists or those maintaining the dispensational view of Israel. Even though the focus here is locating kingdom promises found in the Old Testament, we are in the theological neighborhood of where the discussion of 'Replacement Theology' is a necessity. It cannot be avoided. So, a survey of the theological positions concerning Israel and the church is forthcoming.

First, I am using 'Replacement Theology' as a legitimate theological position, even though numerous scholars and leaders have expressed their displeasure with this term. I totally agree that "Replacement" is not a word that leads to an understanding of how the New Testament answers the Israel/church question. No matter what position on Israel and the church one takes, the term 'Replacement' does not fit within the biblical framework. We do need to replace it. Nevertheless, since it is used by many to describe one of the various positions, it cannot be avoided. No matter how we feel about the term, it is better to face it head on, rather than hide from it. I have heard it said, "I do not believe in replacement theology." Then, when asked to describe their view, they lay out the basic elements that others claim is 'Replacement Theology.'

How should we view Israel? Does the church replace Israel? Does Jesus replace Israel? Does Israel maintain a covenant with God which is separate from Christ? Are the covenants and promises given to Israel in the Old Testament on hold until Jesus returns? Or does the church inherit the promises given to Israel? These are difficult questions, but thankfully, we are not left to sort these matters out without help; the New Testament Apostles wrote extensively on the subject.

Our answers will not come from modern politics, or even a history lesson, but from the exegesis of Scripture. Therefore, I will not be summarizing generations of Israeli history. There will be no discussion of the *Bal-four agreement* or any of the many peace plans. History is necessary to understand modern Israel. And it is important, as the study of any nation is. Yet, that is not our intention here. The focus of this chapter is not modern political Israel, but covenantal Israel as revealed in Scripture and how Israel should be viewed, since the birth of the church.

Various methods of interpretation have been offered over the centuries, to understand Israel and the church. We will examine three proposals, which cover the position of most evangelicals. The first is 'Replacement Theology', which means the church today is the Israel of God and heirs of the Old Testament Promises. The second is 'Separation theology', which is the standard dispensational view, where God has two separate peoples, Israel - the earthly people of God, and the Church - the spiritual people of God. Third, a view called 'Remnant Theology', which carves out a unique alterative position.

Three Views of the Church and Israel

Replacement Theology

Dispensational leaders often write harsh rhetoric about the dangers of 'Replacement Theology'. A quick look at books for sale under the subject 'Replacement Theology' reveal many of these dire warnings.

Ronald E. Depose says, "For over nineteen centuries the Jewish people have been the object of contempt and suspicion. What has been called 'replacement theology' is wildly perceived as being one of the causes of this attitude."[22]

---

[22] Ronald E. Diprose, Israel and the Church-The Origin and Effects of Replacement Theology, Authentic Media, Waynesboro, GA., p. 29

Michael Vlach in his book, *Has the Church Replaced Israel*, states, "I fear that the Supersessionist position is tampering with the strongest biblical evidence possible - multiple explicit declarations in both Testaments that national Israel will be saved and restored."[23]

Bob O'Dell, co-founder of 'Root Source', which is a ministry that provides "access to world-class Jewish biblical teaching online, helping you learn deeper and reach higher in your Christian faith," says, "I firmly believe that God is saying to the churches, that *they must begin moving* in the direction of actively renouncing replacement theology. Or else [they] risk missing out on the next big revival God desires to pour out onto the Christian world."[24]

No one, including myself, wants to miss anything God will do in the future. Yet, according to O'Dell and others, we must be active in 'renouncing replacement theology' to be sure of not missing the next revival. No one wants or should be identified with those responsible for Jewish persecution and "tampering" with the Bible. If I were to write a book strictly on this subject, my title would be, "Replacement Theology - A Biblical Defense" and a subtitle "And Why it is Wrong." How we define our terms is very important. If 'Replacement Theology' can be defined as the church fulfilling Old Testament prophecy – yes, prophecies given to old covenant Israel - count me in. Even despite the accusation of tampering with the clear message of the Bible, as I will attempt to show throughout the following chapters - the message of the New Testament supports the idea that believing Israel (the remnant) and believing gentiles are united by the cross (Ephesians 2;11-22). But, if 'Replacement Theology' is defined as the church stealing promises from old covenant Israel, which Scripture states are their exclusive promises and sees all Jewish people throughout the generations as those people

[23] Michael Vlach, Has the Church Replaced Israel, B&H Publishing Group, Nashville, Tennessee, Introduction

[24] Bob O'Dell, Quoted by Rivkab Lambert Adler, Repentance for Christians In volves Rejecting Replacement Theology, https://www.breakingisraelnews .com/112719/renouncing-replacement-theology/?fbclid=IwAR0z2Z7fzmdIXgC weav2hIQoF71EZmdR1qm4mzrxXXGURh8xsftVXgmgIVY

carrying God's curse on them - count me out. This is not part of what I teach, nor the many others who teach the oneness of Jews and Gentiles by the cross of Jesus. We all can admit prejudice has been a problem in the past, inhuman acts of violence have been perpetuated upon the Jewish people by Christians; we must face the failures of our history. Yet, guilt by association should not prevent the work of continuing biblical study and fresh exegesis on this important subject.

Is 'Replacement Theology' a real and recognized theology? I first opened Allan Cairns *Dictionary of Theological Terms*, to see what a well-respected dictionary of theology has to say. I looked up 'Replacement Theology' and found nothing, not a word. I would have thought there would be an extensive article on the subject. Then I turned to 'Supersessionism,' and found a short article.

Supersessionism According to Alan Cairns

"The derogatory term used especially by Jewish scholars and others involved in Jewish studies, to describe the Biblical belief that the NT Christianity is the fulfillment and completed significance of OT teaching. Statements such as Christ's in John 14:6 or Peter's in Acts 4:12 would be labeled supersessionist. The term is a handy tool to stir up Jewish opposition to the gospel by teaching that Christianity supersedes Judaism."[25]

According to Cairns it is a 'derogatory term', without Biblical support. I can only wonder what would be said about the term 'Replacement Theology'. It seems to me as though it is a popular term used to scare people from considering the subject. Even with that said, there are teological issues at stake. Dispensationalists claim 'Replacement Theology' is the teaching that the "Church replaces Israel."

---

[25] Allan Cairns, Dictionary of Theological Terms, Ambassador Emerald International, Greenville, S.C., 441-442

So, what is 'Replacement Theology' and why are we warned of its dangers? In my search I located several books on the subject and found a Seminary professor who provides a good definition.

Michael J. Vlach, Ph.D. a Professor of Theology at The Master's Seminary in Sun Valley, California, writes about replacement theology.

"The relationship between Israel and the church continues to be a controversial topic. Anyone who has interest in the doctrines of Israel, the church, and the end times, is probably aware of this fact. At the heart of the controversy is the question, Does the church replace, supersede, or fulfill the nation of Israel in God's plan, or will Israel be saved and restored with a unique identity and role? The position that the church is the "new" or "true" Israel that replaces or fulfills national Israel's place in the plan of God has often been called "replacement theology" or "supersessionism." More recently, some have argued for the title "fulfillment theology."[26]

Vlach points out the main points of the discussion. He correctly addresses the different titles and concludes they largely use the same biblical arguments. We can claim, "I do not teach Replacement Theology," but the main points are almost identical to 'Fulfillment Theology' and likewise to "Supersessionism." Although the term *replacement* seems inadequate, it is the term used to describe those who teach that the church - the one new man, created at the cross - enters the Abrahamic, Davidic and New Covenants and walks in the words of the Prophets. If that is the position taken, then the definition of 'Replacement Theology' fits. We may not like it, but until the theological narrative creates a new or altered definition, we need to face it head on. Yes, in a sense it is a derogatory term, but we need to concentrate on the biblical support and exegesis of Scripture and stop attempting to avoid the subject by arguing about which theological term we prefer.

---

[26] Michael J. Vlach, Has The Church Replaced Israel? B&H Publishing Group, Nashville, Tennessee, page, introduction

B.K. Waltke gives us a simple definition of Replacement Theology: "The Jewish nation no longer has a place as the special people of God. That place has been taken by the Christian community, which fulfills God's purpose for Israel."[27]

I like Dr. Vlach's definition better, as it clarifies the issues in more detail. Those who believe "That the church is the "new" or "true" Israel that replaces or fulfills national Israel's place in the plan of God has often been called "replacement theology" or "supersession-ism." More recently, some have argued for the title "fulfillment theology."[28]

I am convinced that the new covenant people - which is a union of Jew and Gentile - are part of the Abrahamic family and inherit the promises. These include the "Blessing of Abraham" and a large number of prophecies found in the Old Testament. As we will see later, Apostle Paul saw the *"Israel of God"* and the "Church" as the same people (Galatians 6:16).

There are slight differences in what dispensationalists say we believe and what those teaching kingdom/new covenant really believe and teach. We are told that in our view Israel has no future in God's plan. That is not true. For those who hold to a 'Victorious eschatology', there is a place of blessing and purpose for every nation. The new covenant does not eliminate nations. True, the current political nation of Israel is not the people of God as in the Old Testament. Old Testament Israel had a covenant with God. After the temple and city were destroyed, the old covenant was no longer valid.

In speaking of a new covenant, he makes the first one obsolete. And what is becoming obsolete and growing old is ready to vanish away. (Hebrews 8:13)

---

[27] B.K. Waltke, Kingdom Promises as Spiritual, page 275

[28] Michael J. Vlach, Has The Church Replaced Israel? B&H Publishing Group, Nashville, Tennessee, page, introduction

By coming up with a new plan, a new covenant between God and his people, God put the old plan on the shelf. And there it stays, gathering dust. (The Message)

This proves that by establishing this new covenant the first is now obsolete, ready to expire, and about to disappear. (The Passion Translation)

God speaks of these new promises, of this new agreement, as taking the place of the old one; for the old one is out of date now and has been put aside forever. (The Living Bible)

Replacement Theology is not 'replacing one people for another', but it is the permeant replacement of the old covenant with the new covenant!

This is Paul's argument in Romans 11 - Israel was not 'rejected', because Paul himself was not rejected and he was a Jew. Jews were given the first opportunity to enter the new covenant. The early church was exclusively Jewish. Now, if individuals rejected Jesus as Israel's Messiah, then they no longer lived within a covenant structure with God. I find no support from the New Testament that Jews could remain under the old covenant and continue their status as the people of God.

The author of Hebrews was careful in choosing the words used to describe the status of the old covenant. When the book of Hebrews was written, the temple in Jerusalem was fully functional. Temple worship according to the Mosaic law, was intact; even though it was over 30 years since the death and resurrection of Jesus. The Jews were practicing their religion even though, unbeknownst to them, God was no longer accepting their sacrifices. Their covenantal structure remained, but the heart of the covenant was "*obsolete*". A few years later, when the temple burned, the old covenant "*disappeared.*"

There is no other choice for Israel or any people group; Christ is the only door into God's kingdom. Yet, those advocating an ever-increasing kingdom and the discipling of nations believe in Israel progressively accepting Jesus - they will be blessed and in time, the nation will reap the benefits. I have hope for the nation of Israel. They had nothing to do with those first-century Jews who rejected Jesus and lost their temple and city in judgment. That generation has come and gone, and they received what Jesus spoke over them.

Fill up, then, the measure of your fathers. You serpents, you brood of vipers, how are you to escape being sentenced to hell? Therefore I send you prophets and wise men and scribes, some of whom you will kill and crucify, and some you will flog in your synagogues and persecute from town to town, so that on you may come all the righteous blood shed on earth, from the blood of righteous Abel to the blood of Zechariah the son of Barachiah, whom you murdered between the sanctuary and the altar. Truly, I say to you, all these things will come upon this generation. (Matthew 23:32-36)

We should not conclude that the judgment Jesus announced on the Israel of his day is a continuing judgment throughout all generations. It was not. Jews and Gentiles today are the same; they are either in covenant with God through Jesus, or they are not. As a political nation, Israel does not have a covenant with God. Also, the United States does not have a covenant with God. There is only one covenant and that is the new covenant. Therefore, all nations can be blessed through what Jesus accomplished in the cross and resurrection.

I support Israel; the nation of Israel and the Israel of God (new covenant church). We should pray for the nation of Israel just like we should pray for all nations. When they act within the international laws and morals, they are to be commended. Likewise, when they violate accepted norms of behavior, they should be condemned, just like any other nation. Israel and all nations have a future and it all depends on their acceptance of Jesus and his offer of the new covenant.

It may surprise many Evangelicals that "Supersessionism", or the newest term - "Replacement Theology" – has been the doctrine of mainline Protestant churches for centuries. It has been the people from the Evangelical Churches that have been greatly influenced by dispensationalism, they maintain a separation between Israel and the church. It is likely because of the eschatology of these denominations; dispensationalists claim "Supersessionism" leaves no place for the current nation of Israel. Most of these denominations are Amillennial in their eschatology, so there is no progressive victory within history. On the other hand, Kingdom eschatology which is more closely linked with Postmillennialism, believes in the discipling of all nations.

What Churches Teach *Supersessionism* or *Replacement Theology*?

According to the Web Page 'Amos 3:7,' this is the list of churches that teach replacement theology or supersessionism:

The United Methodist Church – 8,251,042 Members

Evangelical Lutheran Church in America – 5,038,006 Members

Presbyterian Church (U.S.A.) – 3,407,329 Members

The Lutheran Church – Missouri Synod – 2,512,714 Members

African Methodist Episcopal Church – 2,500,000 Members

The Episcopal Church – 2,333,628 Members

Churches of Christ, Corsicana, Texas – 1,500,000 Members

Greek Orthodox Archdiocese of America – 1,500,000 Members

African Methodist Episcopal Zion Church – 1,430,795 Members

United Church of Christ – 1,330,985 Members

Christian Churches and Churches of Christ, Joplin, Mo. – 1,071,616 Members[29]

This represents millions of Christians who are not supporters of dispensationalism and the doctrine of the two peoples of God, with two different covenants. Along with these traditional Protestant

---

[29] Amos 3:17, https://amos37.com/replacement-denominations/

Churches, there are numerous believers from former Pentecostal/ charismatic churches moving away from the doctrines of dispensationalism. It is easy to spot who is missing from this list. The historic denominations of Pentecostal and Baptist Churches have largely accepted dispensationalism.

In the world of theology, 'Supersessionism' is the term used for what many today call 'Replacement Theology', so we can use either one, since for the most part their Scriptural argument is the same. Since 'Replacement Theology" is used by most in the Evangelical world, this is the term I will use.

Replacement Theology (Supersessionism) can be separated into various subdivisions - punitive, economic and structural.

Punitive Replacement

Israel rejected Jesus as their Messiah. They not only forfeited the kingdom and the Old Testament promises, they were also punished. In this view, God judges Israel. Therefore, the Jews are living under the wrath and judgment of God. By studying "Punitive Super-sessionism" (its official term), I see more clearly why so many are opposed to it. Church history shows a pattern of how this way of thinking can be dangerous. If we think Jews of all generations are cursed by God, this would lead to anti-Semitism. It gives an excuse for our racist attitudes. I and those who hold to forms of victorious eschatology reject this. This is not taught in Scripture.

G. J. Fackre, "The rejection of Christ both eliminates Israel from God's covenant love and provokes divine retribution."[30] The key for this position is that not only did Israel lose their covenant place with God; they also came under 'divine retribution." As we study early church history, we can also find those of this persuasion.

Hippolytus, "And surely you (the Jews) have been darkened in the eyes of your soul with a darkness utter and everlasting."

---

[30] G.J. Fackre, Ecumenical Faith in Evangelical Perspective, Eerdmans, Grand Rapids, Michigan, page 148

Origen, "And we can say with confidence that they (the Jews) will never be restored to their former condition. For they committed a crime of the most unhallowed kind."[31]

This statement by Origen makes us wonder if the Jews of his time, or ours, would repent and regain a relationship with God or not. I agree that the 'former condition' under the Mosaic Law will never be restored, yet, they can always come to Christ and be welcomed into the new covenant.

Lactantius said, that because of the Jews' refusal to repent, God will "bestow the inheritance of eternal life upon foreign nations, and collect to himself a more faithful people out of those who were aliens by birth… on account of these impieties of theirs He cast them off forever."[32]

These words of divine judgment, which will follow Jews of all generations, have been a terrible plight on the church and have contributed to outright prejudice and harmful acts of violence towards the Jews.

Generational Punitive Judgment for Jews is not taught in the Bible.

Yet, we must not avoid the words of Jesus and the many New Testament warnings against first-century Israel. Yes, they were judged. The wrath of God was poured out. This all happened during the years preceding 70 AD. When the end came, the city was destroyed with over 1,000,000 Jews killed and their temple was burned. But we must be clear; the judgment upon Israel ended in 70 AD. After their city and temple were destroyed, from that point on, there is no continuing judgment. Since prejudice has been a problem throughout church history, we must be clear on this.

The concept that all generations of Jews carry the judgment of God violates the new covenant. Jeremiah told us in the context of writing

---

[31] Origen, Against Celsus, 4.22, ANF 7:109

[32] Lactantius, The Divine Institutes, 4.11 ANF 5:220

about the new covenant, that everyone will pay for their own sin (Jeremiah 31:29-30). No longer will the sons pay for the sins of the fathers. All generational curses stop with the coming of the new covenant. Today, God loves Jews and Gentiles alike. The grace of God is being poured out on all people.

With this said, my position is one of 'Limited Punitive Replacement.' God did punish first-century Israel for their rejection of Jesus, but we must always remember and make clear - this judgment came to its end. It is part of history and has no bearing on the present or future. People groups of all races and nations have equal access to the good news of Jesus and his kingdom.

Economic Replacement

Michael J. Vlach: "Economic supersessionism asserts that God planned from the beginning for Israel's role as the people of God to expire with the coming of Christ and the establishment of the church."[33]

V. S. Poythress writes on Israel and Christ: "Because Christ is an Israelite and Christians are in union with Christ, Christians partake of the benefits promised to Israel and Judah in Jeremiah. With whom is the new covenant made? It is made with Israel and Judah. Hence it is made with Christians by virtue of Christ the Israelite. Thus, one might say that Israel and Judah themselves undergo a transformation at the first coming of Christ, because Christ is the final, supremely faithful Israelite. Around him all true Israel gathers."[34]

This version concentrates more on God's eternal plan for Israel as being temporary, rather than focusing on their disobedience and God's judgment. It is a friendly version of *Replacement Theology*. It avoids having to explain the judgment aspects. The problem I see is that both are presented in Scripture. The New Testament authors

---

[33] Michael J. Vlach, Has the Church Replaced Israel, B&H Publishing Group, Nashville, Tennessee, 2010, page 14

[34] V.S. Poythress, Understanding Dispensationalists, 2nd edition, P&R Publishing, Phillipsburg, N.J., 1994, page 106

saw both aspects of God's plan. They saw the change from Israel to the church and the change from the old to the new covenant as God's plan all along. Yet, when Israel rejected Jesus and his offer of the kingdom, they did come under God's judgment.

Structural Replacement

The third form of Replacement Theology is referred to as 'Structural Replacement.' This variety arrives at the same conclusions as the previous two, yet in a different manner. Whereas the previous two positions are theological in nature, this view is based upon hermeneutics. What Structural Replacement does is to devalue the Old Testament as having an equal voice as the New Testament, for Christians.

It is true that we must use proper hermeneutics in understanding the Old Testament. The easiest method may deny its authority as here in Structural Replacement, but that leads to an impoverished church. We must see how the Old Testament enhances the Christian life, not make it disappear by the magic of our hermeneutical hand.

The Old Testament is part of the Christian cannon. We need to learn how to read it through the lens of Christ, not pretend it no longer has anything to say for us living in the new covenant.

The central purpose of "Our Rich Root" is learning to interpret the Old Testament prophetic passages as being fulfilled in Christ and his church. Therefore, a larger theological debate on 'Replacement Theology' is not needed here, as we will view the subject more from the biblical view of exegesis. We will review several Old Testament passages and then read them through the lens of Christ and a New Testament theology.

We must be aware of how terms like 'Replacement Theology' are used and realize they are often used with a pejorative attitude. Nobody wants to steal promises that do not belong to them (as in the church stealing the promises from Israel). For me, there is a larger problem involved - if the church does not fulfill many of the Old Testament prophecies given to the nation Israel, then we must find a different reading of Paul and his apostolic companions, because they, according to my understanding, saw the church as the restored Israel. For them, Jesus reshaped, reorganized and made the Israel of old into the true "Israel of God."

With all these various positions and their sub-divisions, it is time to form some conclusions. I will add the word 'Biblical' in front of 'Replacement Theology' as I attempt to see the Israel/Church relationship flowing naturally from the New Testament. I am not saying my view comes from the Bible and others do not, yet, after reviewing all the options I see a pattern of New Testament theology concerning Israel and the Church which points in the direction of a 'replaced covenant' and a 'renewed people.'

What is Biblical Replacement Theology?

1. Covenantal Replacement

2. God's People Renewed

Our second point highlights the continuity of God's people. God has one people. Even though there was a change of covenant, it did not replace God's call for Israel as defined by the prophets. They were to be the light to the nations. They were to be a blessed people. They were to be the people through which God would bring justice and righteousness. They were to be the people through which God would bring fulfillment. And all this is still true. God never took back his promises to Israel. They have been fulfilled and are being fulfilled.

As the days ended for the Old Testament prophets, a large problem loomed over Israel. They were a backslidden people who had lost their way. Before Israel could be a light to the nations, they had to be revived. Israel had to be renewed. How did this happen? One word. Messiah!

To fix what was wrong with Israel was no easy task. The people needed more than a 'national restoration.' It was time for a true renewal. With the arrival of Jesus and his work through the cross, resurrection and ascension, Israel was at last free from their addiction to rebellion. How? Sin, and the power of darkness were nailed to the cross and defeated.

The other side of this equation is how Israel responded to their Savior and Messiah. It is at this junction that, sad to say, many get confused. One side advocates the renewing of Israel was postponed (until the Second Coming). Others see a complete break and argue for complete discontinuity. They see the Israel of old come to a complete finish - without any fulfillment or renewal. I see the testimony of Jesus and the Apostles pointing to a third way. Israel would be renewed and see her promises fulfilled. Yet, it would take a whole new approach, a new way of relating to the God of Abraham, Isaac and Jacob. With the coming of Jesus, Israel must accept the fact that God had sent him. They must enter the new covenant and be a part of the people of God, centered around the Messiah. A few did; yet, many did not.

The Hope of Israel

Having met with Jewish leaders in Rome, Apostle Paul explained his arrest by stating he was in chains, because of the *"Hope of Israel"* (Acts 28:20). What was the Hope of Israel? Did Jesus and the Apostles make changes to this hope?

The restoration promises for Israel found in the Old Testament prophets were fulfilled in the creation of God's new covenant people. Paul knew his Hebrew Scriptures, he knew the Messianic prophecies, he knew the multitude of promises concerning the ever-increasing kingdom of God and he saw these as being fulfilled in Jesus and through the new people of God. We can read what Paul taught. There should be no question if Paul taught a separate destiny and covenant for natural Israel. He did not. He taught the unity of those in Christ. He taught that because of the cross, all people are now unified. There is only one covenant to find our relationship with God, the new covenant.

Did Apostle Paul teach 'Replacement Theology'? According to those who use the term; Yes. Yet, we must again bring up that this term is inadequate to express what Paul and the New Testament authors had to say on the subject. Nevertheless, the letters of Paul express what he taught, and he called it the 'Hope of Israel.'

Israel's hope for generations was that God would come and be their king. This is exactly what happened in the incarnation of the son of God. Jesus came to fulfill what the Prophet Zechariah spoke. Their king was coming!

Rejoice greatly, O daughter of Zion! Shout aloud, O daughter of Jerusalem! Behold, your king is coming to you; righteous and having salvation is he, humble and mounted on a donkey, on a colt, the foal of a donkey. (Zechariah 9:9)

I will continue to provide support for what I call, 'Biblical Replacement Theology' in the next chapter. It is the theology of dispensationalism where much of the heated rhetoric about 'stealing' Israel's promises and 'tampering' with the Bible comes.

Chapter 8
Israel and the Church - Separation Theology

Biblical 'Replacement Theology' sees Christ and his church as fulfilling the promises given to natural Israel. *Separation Theology* is the opposite. It is the doctrine of Dispensationalism. It keeps Israel and the church separate. They have different promises, abide by different covenants, and have a different future. This creates two peoples of God, which continue into eternity. Today, the dispensational doctrine of Israel is seen in 'Christian Zionism'. Zionism is a Jewish political movement that claims the Jewish people have a 'divine' right to the land of Palestine. Christian Zionism supports this position and endorses the doctrine that the modern state of Israel is the same as biblical Israel.

Since I wrote extensively on the failures of Dispensational Eschatology in my book, *Glorious Kingdom*, I will not repeat those arguments here. Yet, there is one passage by Apostle Paul, that causes sharp divisions about what is the intended meaning of 'Israel'; Paul's words in Galatians 6. Dispensationalists repeatedly claim, "The church is never called Israel" and therefore, these words need to be explored in depth.

For neither circumcision counts for anything, nor uncircumcision, but a new creation. And as for all who walk by this rule, peace and mercy be upon them, and upon the Israel of God. (Galatians 6:15-16)

I see a pattern in what Paul wrote that I noticed in his letter to the Romans. In Romans 14 he writes rules concerning what to eat and drink. I can imagine, after writing how believers should behave, he needed a break, being maybe a little frustrated, because he would rather get to the heart of what Jesus had done for us, which was much more than giving us a new set of rules. Suddenly, a wave of Holy Spirit inspiration comes upon him and he writes, "*For the kingdom of God is not a matter of eating and drinking but of righteousness and peace and joy in the Holy Spirit. Whoever thus serves Christ is acceptable to God and approved by men (Romans 14:17-18").* This is Apostle Paul at his finest! With a few words he wraps up a long debate on how Christians should live and keys to what is vital to their faith.

I sense something like that is happening here in Galatians 6. Paul has made several convincing arguments throughout his letter, most of them explaining about God's single family, which goes back to Abraham. He deals with the contested issue of circumcision and then again, in a moment of brilliant inspiration, he summarizes everything in verse 16. His conclusion is simple, 'Get circumcised, don't get circumcised, those things matter little'. What is important is the 'new creation.' This is how we should walk.

Before seeing our interpretive options for the "Israel of God", a quick review of how circumcision was seen in the first century may be helpful.

Paul wrote that neither 'circumcision', nor 'uncircumcision', was the point of what God was doing. For us who are far removed from first-century Jewish culture, this does not seem to raise a major issue; but as we read throughout the New Testament, both sides of the issue are hotly contested.

Circumcision was part of the Mosaic Law. It was a mark of being Jewish, part of being a member of ancient Israel - the chosen people of God.

In the Greek culture - the prominent secular culture in Judea of the first century - circumcision was viewed as 'not civilized'. In an article, Michael Glass explains the Greek attitude.

"The New Testament comes from a multicultural background. It is, of course, grounded in the Jewish religion. Jews circumcised their boys on their eighth day of life and regarded this rite as essential (Genesis 17:9-14). However, it was written in Greek, and was therefore immersed in the Greek culture, which, at the time, was dominant in that part of the Roman Empire. These two great cultures came together in the New Testament. There were, of course, many points of convergence between them both, but there were some notable clashes. One was over circumcision."[35]

Glass continues and states that within the Greek culture, a man could participate in "public games" completely naked, as long as he was 'covered,' which meant if he was not circumcised.[36] As odd as this seems today, circumcision was significant in their cultures, both in the secular Greek and the religious Jewish culture.

With both Jewish and Greek cultures placing importance on circumcision, Paul would have a difficult time explaining why 'circumcision' was no longer significant. He was confronting his own people and the very commandment of God. The authors of the New Testament, and especially Paul, knew circumcision was an issue that had to be dwelt with, precisely because of its theological implications.

For freedom Christ has set us free; stand firm therefore, and do not submit again to a yoke of slavery. Look: I, Paul, say to you that if you accept circumcision, Christ will be of no advantage to you. I testify again to every man who accepts circumcision that he is obligated to keep the whole law. (Galatians 5:1-3)

If anyone was thinking that circumcision would help save them, then, Paul made it clear - circumcision would lead them back to slavery. The gospel, according to Paul, was that the work of Jesus is what saves, and not the law. In his letter to the believers living in Colossae, he wrote about the true work of circumcision.

In him also you were circumcised with a circumcision made without hands, by putting off the body of the flesh, by the circumcision of Christ. (Colossians 2:11)

---

[35] Michael Glass, *The New Testament and Circumcision*. October 2001, http://www.cirp.org/pages/cultural/glass1/

[36] Ibid.

Look out for the dogs, look out for the evildoers, look out for those who mutilate the flesh. For we are the circumcision, who worship by the Spirit of God and glory in Christ Jesus and put no confidence in the flesh. (Philippians 3:2-3)

Paul is very clear on this issue. Our trust and faith must be in Christ Jesus. Therefore, in Galatians 6, Paul again teaches that circumcision is not important, and it is dangerous for anyone trusting in the old Laws instead of trusting Christ. What is imperative is not the keeping of the Laws but being a "new creation."

Paul refers to 'do not trust circumcision, but the new creation in Christ' as a rule, a truth, which had to be followed so the blessings of God could be obtained.

And as for all who walk by this rule, peace and mercy be upon them, and upon the Israel of God (Gal. 6:16).

What does "Israel of God" mean? The doctrinal differences in understanding the relationship between Israel and the church can be traced in part to this verse. There are at least three options for interpreting what Paul meant by "Israel of God."

Option One: The 'Israel of God' is the 'Jewish Believers'

The first option is that the phrase "Israel of God" refers to 'Jewish Believers'. In reviewing several translations, I found the Amplified Bible - which I normally find helpful -capitulate to interpretation of this difficult verse.

Peace and mercy be upon all who walk by this rule [who discipline themselves and conduct their lives by this principle], and upon the [true] Israel of God (Jewish believers). (Amplified Bible)

Here the translator gives his opinion on the key question of who 'Israel' represents. He says it is 'Jewish believers.' If this is true, it is a departure, not only from Paul's understanding of the family of God, but other apostolic authors of the New Testament as well. Their arguments, as I read them, are a consistent voice, that 'in Christ' God has created one family. Not a family with various sub-divisions. Not a family made of Jewish Christians and yet another from Gentile Christians. If this is what Paul had in mind, he strays from his own doctrine that in Christ there is no Jew or Gentile (Galatians 2:28). His whole argument is against such divisions in the flesh that separate people who are in Christ. I do not see this as a viable option because it goes contrary to the overall message of the Apostle.

Paul's conclusion may be said like this, "If you want the "peace and mercy" of God, it is only available to those of the "new creation." Then Paul adds what may be one of the most contentious words in the New Testament; "*And upon the Israel of God.*" The Amplified version gives us the first option. The "Israel of God" is the 'Jewish believers.'

Option Two: The 'Israel of God' is ethnic Israel

The option taken by dispensationalists is that the phrase "Israel of God" means the Old Testament people of God; national Israel. They claim Paul is separating those of the 'new creation' from the nation of Israel. There are two groups of people in verse 16. One is Jewish and the other - Christians. Therefore, since Israel as a nation rejected the offer of the kingdom by Jesus, the kingdom promises and their covenants will be fulfilled only after the Second Coming of Christ in the millennial kingdom. The church, according to this option, is never seen, spoken of, or the recipient of any Old Testament prophecy.

Option Three: "The Israel of God" and the "Church" are the same people.

This third option is not popular in many parts of western Evangelic-alism. This is the position I embrace. When Paul writes about the "Israel of God" in Galatians 6, it is the Christians (Jews and Gentiles) that make up the people of the '*new creation.*' The "*Israel of God*" refers to those in the church, all who have been redeemed and transformed through the Spirit and by the work of Christ. The term *"Israel of God"* and the "church" are interchangeable; they are the same. Can a case be made for this interpretation?

I will freely admit, when it comes to rightly interpreting a highly contested verse in Scripture, and especially a single word, it is beyond my exegetical paygrade. In N.T. Wright's massive two-volume book, *Paul and the Faithfulness of God*, he took six pages on Galatians 6:16 and the question of Israel. I would love my readers to have access to his exegesis as it is fair, thorough, detailed, and in my mind, brilliant. Yet, to quote all six pages would be unethical, maybe illegal, and for sure unfair to Professor Wright. To read his complete exegesis on this key verse, you need to buy all 2,200 pages. Nevertheless, I will quote Wright on his interpretation of the word, 'Israel', and give a few highlights of his conclusion.

N.T. Wright: "Obviously, then, if Paul were to use "Israel" in this passage to mean 'the whole seed of Abraham, believing Jews and believing Gentiles together', this would constitute a seriously polemical redefinition. But that is hardly foreign either to his practice in general or to the present passage in particular."[37]

Wright does not avoid the difficult questions or the implications that his conclusions will bring. A detailed reading of Paul's letters shows that he is not averse to redefining traditional concepts and being outright controversial when it comes to revealing the radical changes brought about by Jesus and the new covenant. So, for him to use the term *"Israel of God"* and apply it to all believers in the Messiah is not the leap a student of Scripture should be fearful of taking. It is rather the opposite interpretation, namely that the *"Israel of God"* is a separate group from those of the *'new creation'*, that would be a huge redefining of Paul's theology.

Wright continues: "All this points us on, from earlier moments of the letter, to the highly probably reading of the additional phrase 'of God' in 6.16b. "The Israel of God, in light of the letter so far, *must* mean 'the household of faith' (6.10), those who walk according to

---

[37] N.T. Wright, Paul and The Faithfulness of God, Fortress Press, Minneapolis, 2013, page 1146

the rule of new creation as opposed to that of 'circumcision/ uncircumcision' (6.15), and so on. Paul is talking precisely about an 'Israel' not defined by sarx, 'flesh', but by the Messiah in whom the grace of God has been embodied (2.19-21)."[38]

The following quote from Wright is addressing the implications of the view that the "Israel of God" and those of the 'new creation' are two separate groups.

"But if it were the case that Paul suddenly at this late stage, meant something else by 'God's Israel' - meant, for instance, to refer either to all Jews, or to all Christian Jews, or to some subset of either of those whether now or in the future then he would, quite simply, have made nonsense of the whole letter. Why write Galatians 3 and 4, if that was where it was going to end up? Why not settle for two families, two 'inheritances', instead of a single one?[39]

This is a strong argument for a single group. For Paul, to create two separate groups at the end of his letter, without any explanation, would bring into question his previous statements.

The conclusion of Wright and one which I wholeheartedly endorse, is that Paul was writing about a single group.

"It has been argued forcibly that this passage, and similar passages elsewhere in scripture and second-temple literature, were being echoed by Paul at this point, and that this, granted Paul's other use of the same passages, makes a further strong case for seeing the 'Israel of God' in 6,16b not as a separate entity, but precisely as the believing church."[40]

---

[38] Ibid.

[39] N.T. Wright, Paul and The Faithfulness of God, Fortress Press, Minneapolis, 2013, page 1151

[40] Ibid.

The "Israel of God" and the "Church" are the same people!

This should not surprise us, as we have ample evidence that the Apostolic authors included Gentile believers within the family of Abraham and as heirs to the promises. We see this throughout the New Testament (Romans 4:16, Galatians 3:29, Galatians 4:26,28, Ephesians 2:12, 19, Philippians 3:3, I Peter 2:11).

In my view both the "Jewish believers" option and the dispensational option misrepresent the teachings of the New Testament. They create more exegetical and theological problems than they attempt to solve. It has been harmful to the church and must be faithfully resisted. In the Kingdom of God there is one people of God, there is one family of Abraham, and it is the church of Jesus Christ.

Chapter 9
Israel and Remnant Theology

Remnant Theology is not well-known but provides a different viewpoint than the previous two. John J. Parsons wrote an article called, *Israel and the Church - Understanding Some Theological Options.*[41] In this article he makes an argument for what he calls 'Remnant Theology.' Although I appreciate that Parsons brings out Apostle Paul's discussion in Romans 11, his conclusions are different from what I proposed, and he points us in a rather peculiar direction.

What is *Remnant Theology*? Romans 11 is interpreted with the idea that the Gentiles are grafted into the Remnant of Israel. This is a good beginning. But he goes in a direction I don't believe Paul had in mind. Since the church is grafted into a subset of Israel the church must identify with the remnant, or, can I say, Jewish culture. This Jewish remnant remains to this day as there have always been Jewish believers since the day of Pentecost. The problem I see in this 'Remnant Theology' view of Israel and the Church is that Gentiles are to act and take on Jewish culture.

Parson defends his view, "One consequence of this perspective is that Gentile Christians must return to the Jewish roots of their faith and show love and appreciation for Israel."[42]

If we ask, "Why must we return to our Jewish roots", Parson answers, "Because we consider them our 'eschatological brethren.'

---

[41] John J. Parsons, Israel and the Church-Understanding some Theological Options, http://www.hebrew4christians.com/Articles/Israel/israel.html

[42] John J. Parsons, Israel and the Church-Understanding some Theological Options, http://www.hebrew4christians.com/Articles/Israel/israel.html

The secular state of Israel is actually a part of the end-times theater of operation."[43]

Should Gentiles become like Jews? Parson gives the view of 'Remnant Theology.' "The Gentile Church shouldn't call faithful Jews away from their heritage, but rather should seek to embrace Jewish heritage as its own."[44]

I agree that we need to return to our ancient roots found in the Old Testament. That has been my argument from the beginning. Yet, that is not how Parson views it. He sees a return to the customs and traditions of what it is to be Jewish. It remains unclear how that would look. In the end, this view is a sub-group of standard dispensationalism that places the secular state of Israel as part of the 'end-times.'

What can be said about this trend of Christians dressing and taking on cultural tokens from Judaism? Stop it! This is the kind of activity, which Apostle Paul addressed 2,000 years ago, and we battle with the same today. Paul did not have to debate about wearing hats or carrying prayer shawls, but about the food, drink and circumcision. He concluded that people trusting in these types of visible signs had fallen from grace (Galatians 5:3-4). How can a new covenant believer think they are getting closer to God and his purposes on the earth by dressing like modern Jews (especially Hasidic), or worse - dressing like Jews from the middle ages? Of course, most of these Christians do not dress like Hasidic Jews but pick and choose a few items to wear. I would agree with Apostle Paul; if you are going to travel down that path; if you want to identify with old covenant Israel, go all the way and dress in the proper fashion.

Of the three choices presented here, at least how we are defining it, *Replacement Theology* represents the teachings of Jesus and the Apostles most accurately. No one likes the term, but the biblical

---

[43] Ibid.

[44] Ibid

argument for something like 'Replacement Theology' must be made at some point. One thing is clear, there is no group called the 'Gentile church'. The church has never consisted of only Gentiles. So, if we define 'Replacement Theology' as the Gentile church replacing Israel, we begin with a history, which is not true. If we say the church of the new covenant, made up of Jews and Gentiles, replaces the nation of Israel with its Mosaic Covenant", then, yes, something is being replaced. The people remain the same; it is the covenants which are being replaced. We - the people of the new covenant - are neither Jews, nor Gentiles - we are a new creation, the one new man, which is the body of Christ.

Our task in this book is not to weigh too deeply into this subject of replacement or not but to see how the revelation of the kingdom of God comes from both the Old and New Testaments. Therefore, we must return to the words and visions of the Prophets to gain a full vision of what is available to those of us living in the kingdom.

Even though the term "Replacement Theology" is used mostly in a pejorative way, and some definitions are flawed, it remains the closest to what is presented by Apostle Paul and the rest of the New Testament authors.

The best place to begin is with the New Testament authors, so we can see how they used terms taken from old covenant Israel and applied them to the church.

Who gave himself for us to redeem us from all lawlessness and to purify for himself a people for his own possession who are zealous for good works. (Titus 2:14)

When Apostle Paul uses the phrase "*A people for his own possession*" he is connecting the new covenant people with the same words God refers to old Israel.

*Now then, if you will indeed obey My voice and keep My covenant, then you shall be **My own possession** among all the peoples, for all the earth is Mine; and you shall be to Me a kingdom of priests and* *a holy nation.' These are the words that you shall speak to the sons of Israel."* (Exodus 19:5-6 (NASB)

*For you are a holy people to the LORD your God; the LORD your God has chosen you to be a people for **His own possession** out of all the peoples who are on the face of the earth.* (Deuteronomy 7:6 (NASB)

Why would Paul, along with other New Testament authors, use the same language for old covenant Israel and the church? The obvious answer, at least it should be, is because of the close connection between Israel and the church. The church is grafted into the covenants and promises God originally gave Israel. Since the death and resurrection of Jesus the church is the *"people of God's possession"*.

But you are a chosen race, a royal priesthood, a holy nation, a people for his own possession, that you may proclaim the excellencies of him who called you out of darkness into his marvelous light. Once you were not a people, but now you are God's people; once you had not received mercy, but now you have received mercy. (I Peter 2:9-10)

If the church interrupts God's plan for Israel, why would these passages be extremely clear in making the connection that those who are 'in Christ' are God's present people and carry the same designations of old covenant Israel? Peter calls Christians *"A chosen race,"* *"A royal priesthood,"* *"A holy nation,"* and then repeats the phrase Paul used, *"A people for his own possession."* All these terms were used for Israel throughout the Old Testament. These labels were used only for Israel as they were the covenant people of God among the nations. So is the church! We are the chosen race, the holy priesthood and the holy nation. How did this happen? Because of God's mercy. We were once not a people, but now we are.

Oswald T. Allis wrote a book in 1945, titled, *Prophecy and The Church*, which should have been a death sentence to dispensationalism. I do not know of any dispensational scholar that has come close to refuting the exegesis and theological conclusions of Allis. His comments of I Peter 2:9 are worth reading.

"That this use of, or reference to, the language of the Pentateuch is intentional can hardly be questioned. Consequently, the question is this, Do Paul and Peter use this expression for the purpose of calling attention to the close and vital connection which exists between Old Testament Israel and the New Testament Church? Or, do they expect us to understand that there are two 'peculiar peoples," which are to be carefully distinguished?"[45]

Allis asks an important question. Are there now, in the present, two peoples? Does God the Father possess Israel as his people, while Jesus possesses the church for his people? The answer is, "No". There is no Gentile church, as there is no Jewish church, or European, or American church. The church is made up of Jews and Gentiles, therefore is not known by the ethnicity of its members. There is only one people of God. Paul makes this abundantly clear in the second chapter of Ephesians.

Remember that you were at that time separated from Christ, alienated from the commonwealth of Israel and strangers to the covenants of promise, having no hope and without God in the world. (Ephesians 2:12)

Paul is speaking to Gentiles and according to his understanding, they were not part of the 'commonwealth of Israel' and had no part of the covenants of promise. What is the *"commonwealth of Israel?"* And what are the *"covenants of promise?"*

First, as in Hebrew parallelism (where the author will repeat the same concept with different words) the second phrase is part of the definition. *The covenants of promise* make up the foundation to what is to be considered *the commonwealth of Israel.* Notice it is 'covenants' - plural, not singular. I would see this as referring to the Abrahamic, Davidic and New Covenant. Therefore, those in the

---

[45] Oswald T. Allis, Prophecy and The Church, The Presbyterian and Reformed Publishing Company, page 55

commonwealth of Israel, are 'citizens' of Israel and possess the rights that are shared by all within that group.

If we can define being part of a 'commonwealth', as being a 'citizen,' then, we can make the following conclusion of what Paul is teaching: those Gentiles, who are now being brought into Christ, are 'citizens' of Israel. They have been brought close to all that is available in the 'commonwealth.'

Now the elephant in the room needs to be addressed. Through their relationship with Christ, the Gentiles are included in the *commonwealth of Israel.* Paul is clear about that. What about the Jews who rejected Jesus as their Messiah? Do they remain part of this 'commonwealth', with the newly added Gentiles? Does the New Testament teach the physical descendants of Israel can remain part of this 'commonwealth', while rejecting Jesus as their Messiah? No! Over and over, Jesus and the apostles teach the imperative of accepting Jesus as the one whom God sent.

In the four gospels this subject came up numerous times. The first time was with John the Baptist.

In those days John the Baptist came preaching in the wilderness of Judea, "Repent, for the kingdom of heaven is at hand. (Matthew 3:1-2)

The context is the preaching of the kingdom. John was announcing the arrival of Israel's Messiah and the coming of God's kingdom. Although this should have been 'good news' to the Jews, it would require 'repentance.' The Jews of the day were not being called to make a list of their personal failures, but to 'change their mind' concerning the true ministry of their Messiah and the nature of God's kingdom.

Now, back to Paul's argument in Ephesians.

But now in Christ Jesus you who once were far off have been brought near by the blood of Christ. (Ephesians 2:13)

Through Christ, we, who were 'far off' (disconnected from the *commonwealth of Israel*) are now brought near. Near to what? We are now included in Israel's covenantal promises.

For he himself is our peace, who has made us both one and has broken down in his flesh the dividing wall of the law of commandments expressed in ordinances, that hostility by abolishing he might create in himself one new man in place of the two, so making peace. (Ephesians 2:14-15)

The Scripture declares, "*made us both one.*" There can be no division between Jews and Gentiles, if they are in Christ. The wall of division has been broken down and now, according to Paul, there is "*one new man*" replacing the two.

Paul concludes this section by reminding us of the benefits of being part of this new man.

So then you are no longer strangers and aliens, but you are fellow citizens with the saints and members of the household of God. (Ephesians 2:19)

Those 'in Christ' are the saints and members of God's house. With the coming of Jesus and his kingdom, there was only one way to be included - accept Jesus as the Christ. This is the context of what Jesus teaches in John 10.

Truly, truly, I say to you, he who does not enter the sheepfold by the door but climbs in by another way, that man is a thief and a robber. But he who enters by the door is the shepherd of the sheep. To him the gatekeeper opens. The sheep hear his voice, and he calls his own sheep by name and leads them out. (John 10:1-3)

The context is showing us that being a physical descendant of Israel does not allow one to enter God's blessing, apart from entering the proper door. Who are the 'thieves', who attempt to enter God's field from a different door? They are primarily the Jews, who maintain they can reject Jesus and remain in the house. The door is Jesus and in him we have abundant life. Any person, group, or religion, which claims a different door to God, is false. There is no other door.

The thief comes only to steal and kill and destroy. I came that they may have life and have it abundantly. (John 10:10)

I have heard many times that this verse is about Satan, the 'thief'. Yet, Jesus already told us who the 'thief' was. The 'thief' is the people attempting to enter God's household a different way rather than through him. This is not a word about Satan nor does the context allow for such an interpretation. Jesus tells us who the thief is, there is no reason to change it.

Chapter 10
The Hope of Israel

The church is the result of the '*Hope of Israel.*' Who we are as God's people is what the prophets foretold. Now, there was a serious misunderstanding among the people of Israel, because they thought their Messiah would be a warrior king like David, who would kill off their enemies. Therefore, doctrines like dispensationalism still claim an Old Testament type of a kingdom is what God wants. Yet, Jesus in his three years of teaching was clear about the type of kingdom he was bringing.

The prophets spoke of this new type of kingdom, but there are also passages wrapped in Old Testament covenantal language where it seems the Messiah's reign would follow the same pattern. This is where a Christocentric hermeneutic is so important, because it allows Jesus to define the nature of his kingdom and allows us to return to those passages in the Old Testament and read them again, in the knowledge of what Jesus taught.

For this reason, therefore, I have asked to see you and speak with you, since it is because of the hope of Israel that I am wearing this chain. (Acts 28:20)

Apostle Paul was a prisoner of the empire; and having arrived in Rome he met with the Jewish leaders. In his conversation he made an astonishing statement. He said the purpose for his arrest and the reason for his chains was because he was preaching the "*Hope of Israel.*" Did Paul say that right? Maybe he should have said, "For the hope of the Gentiles, I was arrested." No, Paul knew exactly what he was saying, and he understood the deep meaning behind the words. The "*Hope of Israel*" is only found in Christ. It is not only the hope for the Jews, but for all peoples and all nations. The "*Hope of Israel*" is Jesus and his kingdom. This was the message of Paul. Those who were the physical seed of Abraham had to come to Christ; this was their only hope, as it remains today for all.

The doctrines and teachings of Paul are well known. We have them and they are part of our New Testament cannon. If Paul was preaching an 'Israel only' kingdom or an old covenant type kingdom, we would know. He did not. What did Paul teach about Israel and the Messiah's kingdom? There are people, who espouse Jesus preached the kingdom of God, but Paul preached justification by faith – that is, a different message. It is true, that Paul uses the word "kingdom" less than Jesus, but his mission was much different. Jesus came to announce the kingdom and establish it through his death and resurrection. He attempted to show the Jews of his day how this 'kingdom' would look and how it operated. Once Jesus had ascended back into heaven, it was Paul who took up the task of explaining the meaning behind everything. Paul did not write a single letter, at least among those in the New Testament, until 20 to 25 years after Jesus was crucified.

What was the *"Hope of Israel?"* It depended on who you asked. If we had lived in first-century Jerusalem and asked the religious leaders, we would have gotten a different answer than if we asked Peter on the day of Pentecost. Now, we should not be overly wrought about the many Jews who misunderstood the coming reign of Jesus; even most of his disciples got it wrong. It was not until the Spirit was poured out, that the lights of revelation were turned on.

The Hope of Israel from an Old Covenant Perspective

Arriving at an old covenant view of the *"Hope of Israel"* is simple - we just read the Old Testament as if the New Testament was never written. When we come across passages that look, "New Covenant", we read them again and fit them into the old covenant pattern. Of course, all this is backwards and a poor method of interpreting the Scripture. Yet, it is being done to this day.

The Hope of Israel from a New Covenant Perspective

Despite the overwhelming support for the *"Hope of Israel"* being found within the old covenant structure, it is only to be found by recognizing that by the death and resurrection of Jesus, everything changed. Yes, everything! First, it made the old covenant obsolete. Therefore, any attempt to pattern the kingdom of Jesus according to old covenant is dead on arrival. At least it should be.

We will begin in the Gospels. We have several individuals making statements about God's intentions, in their lifetime.

Now there was a man in Jerusalem, whose name was Simeon, and this man was righteous and devout, waiting for the consolation of Israel, and the Holy Spirit was upon him. And it had been revealed to him by the Holy Spirit that he would not see death before he had seen the Lord's Christ. And he came in the Spirit into the temple, and when the parents brought in the child Jesus, to do for him according to the custom of the Law, he took him up in his arms and blessed God and said, "Lord, now you are letting your servant depart in peace, according to your word for my eyes have seen your salvation that you have prepared in the presence of all peoples, a light for revelation to the Gentiles, and for glory to your people Israel." (Luke 2: 25-32)

Simeon was *"Waiting for the consolation of Israel."*

And there was a prophetess, Anna, the daughter of Phanuel, of the tribe of Asher. She was advanced in years, having lived with her husband seven years from when she was a virgin, and then as a widow until she was eighty-four, She did not depart from the temple, worshiping with fasting and prayer night and day. And coming up at that very hour she began to give thanks to God and to speak of him to all who were waiting for the redemption of Jerusalem. (Luke 2:36-38)

We have two individuals, Simeon and Anna who were 'waiting' for God to accomplish what he had promised. They had expectations that they would live to see it. If Anna lived longer, she would have been a follower of Jesus, experiencing the powerful 'Baptism in the Holy Spirit' and coming to a place where she would have understood that the 'old Jerusalem' had to be removed so that the 'Jerusalem from above' could be revealed.

The "*Hope of Israel*" is the hope of all humanity. It is the reign of Jesus over the world. It is his people experiencing the grace and love of God and being those who reflect Gods image to all creation.

Chapter 11
Corporate Christology

How can we say, 'All is fulfilled in Christ' and separate the church from any of the benefits? What may be missing is the degree to which Jesus and his church are connected. Apostle Paul uses the phrase, *"In Christ"* throughout his letters, to show how Christians are not just following the teachings of Jesus, but are one with him, through the ministry of the Spirit.

Although the title of this chapter is "Corporate Christology", the phrase "Incorporated into Christ" is another phrase that may be used to describe the work of the Spirit in bringing the new believer into the presence of the resurrected Christ. We are joined to Christ in a union, which is beyond our human metaphors and symbols.

Christ is the head of the church. We are his body. In human terms, what the head (our brain) instructs, the body performs. In order for our fingers to move, the instructions must travel from our head to our fingers so that they can perform the action. It happens so fast it seems the fingers have their own power to move individually (independent of the head), but they don't. This is a human analogy of what takes place between Christ and his spiritual body - the church. How can Christ fulfill prophecy separate from the church?

One argument that can view Christ as an individual fulfilling prophecy is to look at his birth, baptism, unique suffering and death, as well as at other aspects of his life, and say it would be hard to see the church experiencing them in a way which can be classified as 'fulfilled prophecy.' Even though in the past, and even today, some people are looking for an interpretation by using 'allegory' as their interpretative method. In my mind, in many of these cases it goes too far. Yes, the church does suffer; yes, the church can be likened to a pure virgin, etc., but I would conclude there are many Old Testament prophecies that exclusively refer to the life of Jesus while he was on earth and should not be 'pressed' to include the church.

Here are Old Testament passages which prophesy about aspects of the life of Jesus and should not necessarily include the church in some mystical fashion.

His Virgin Birth: Micah 5:2

He would be a Prophet like Moses: Deuteronomy 18:15

He would enter the gates triumphal: Zechariah 9:9

He would be rejected: Isaiah 53:1,3

He would be betrayed for 30 pieces of silver: Zechariah 11:12-13

He would be silent before his accusers: Isaiah 53:7-8

He would die by crucifixion: Psalm 22:14-16

His garments would be divided: Psalm 22:18

Am I arguing against my own position? Even though these passages are not fulfilled by the church (because they foretold historical events fulfilled by Jesus), there are multitudes of other Old Testament prophecies where the church is seen as the beneficiary.

We need to go beyond the prophetic words of the Messiah to include a plethora of passages about his kingdom. Once Jesus came, he accomplished what needed to be done on earth, he was given *'dominion, glory, and a kingdom'* from the Father (Daniel 7:13-14). He now reigns as King over all creation and He has a special relationship with the church - his body. The tendency to group all Old Testament prophecies together and declare them all 'Fulfilled in Christ" fails to recognize the ministry of the church in advancing the kingdom by its union with its head - King Jesus!

Corporate Christology

When Jesus ascended into heaven, he was brought before the courts of heaven and given the kingdom (Daniel 7:14). The Prophets had much to say about the Messiah as King. It is our union with the head - King Jesus, that provides the way for the church to enter into the ministry of 'kingdom advancement'.

How does the New Testament express the union of Christ and the church?

1. He is the head and we are the body (I Corinthians 12:12).

2. He is the bridegroom and we are the bride.

3. He is the foundation stone and we are the building blocks of living stones.

4. He is the Vine and we are the Branches (John 15:5).

5. We are in Christ (Philippians 1:1, II Corinthians 5:17, Ephesians 1:22).

Without this connection to our roots, the church is in danger of lapsing into passivity. "Everything is fulfilled, I have Jesus and the Holy Spirit so what more do I need?" Since we already discounted all Old Testament kingdom prophecies, we now look for ways to lessen the impact of our responsibility. We turn the 'Great Commission (Matt, 28:18-19)' into a suggestion beyond the reach of the church, or we claim it was fulfilled when the Jewish temple was destroyed, or we deceive ourselves by thinking, "God will disciple the nations without our help." The church is not called to be a selfish group of individuals that are unconcerned about the world. Have all the personal 'spiritual experiences' you can get but if they leave you without passion to reach the world and don't move you to help others, it is time to question what kind of spirit you are experiencing.

As we have mentioned, in his letters Apostle Paul makes numerous references to the words "*In Christ*." The first-century Christians who knew about Paul's doctrines would have been aware of this. When Paul writes about the olive tree in Romans 11, he is not framing his thoughts on how the church is incorporated into Christ, but rather, how the church is "Incorporated into Israel." This is Paul's whole argument going back to the ninth chapter, explaining the relationship between Israel and those now who are now "*In Christ*."

For the Christians in Rome who were mostly Gentiles, this was important. Living at the center of the Empire, it would be easy to think that God had made "Us" his chosen people and Israel was no longer important on any level. Paul made it clear that the Gentiles were grafted into Israel, not the other way around. They were connected to Israel; not through their present rebellion, but through the rich roots of being a part of Abraham's family.

Conclusion to Section 1
Drawing from Our Rich Root

With the abundance of words it is possible to lose sight of the primary objective, which is locating and interpreting the Old Test-ament prophecies and applying them to the church. Since, in my opinion, there are many passages which are prophetic for the church, a list of the key promises will be useful.

1. The church will be the people of God

2. The Spirit will be poured out on the church

3. The church will receive a new covenant

4. The church will possess nations

5. Through the church righteousness will increase

6. Through the church worship and praise will fill the earth

7. The hand of God's blessing will be on the church

8. The church's destiny is to love God and to celebrate in his kingdom.

What are the practical applications of this connection to the prophets? Why is it important for the contemporary church?

- **We maintain the integrity of the Bible**

All the Bible, both the Old and New Testaments, is useful to the new covenant believers. Even though parts are not binding (Mosaic Law), they remain part of the inspired (God breathed) Scripture.

Jay Rogers is on target when he states, "The Old Testament is rife with prophecies concerning the nations being under Christ the Messiah. This is an important aspect of our faith. A whole book would be necessary to quote entirely the texts of the Old Testament, that predict the triumph to come in Christ and how all the nations shall be His."[46]

Maintaining the integrity of the Bible would include the Apostolic Hermeneutic, which upholds that the new covenant is the final covenant and that it supersedes all previous covenants. All covenants are progressive, having their end in the new covenant.[47]

All Scripture is breathed out by God and profitable for teaching, for reproof, for correction, and for training in righteousness, that the man of God may be complete, equipped for every good work. (II Timothy 3:16-17)

When Paul states "*All Scripture*" he is referring to all of the Old Testament.

By applying an Apostolic Interpretation:

- We maintain a Biblical vision for the Kingdom.
- We interpret the Prophets by ALL of God's story, which is finalized in the New Testament.
- We are freed to interpret the Old Testament in a 'biblical' method and not restricted to a false 'literal' hermeneutic.
- We gain valuable insight from the Old Testament Prophets.
- We can manage our gifts and talents to work with the promise of the kingdom.
- We are building hope and a sense of destiny for the Church.

---

[46] Jay Rogers, The Postmillennial view, http://www.forerunner.com/eschatology/X0001_1._Postmil.html, 2008

[47] Peter J. Gentry, Stephen J. Wellum, Kingdom through Covenant, Crossway, Wheaton, Illinois, 2012

Apostolic Interpretation

Rule No.1

Examine the context to determine if a passage is fulfilled within Old Testament History.

We first look at the context. Normal principles of hermeneutics are not tossed out, that's where we begin. Yet this can be tricky, because, as you will observe, most Old Testament passages have their primary context within their 'time and history' yet within the passage there is 'new covenant' truth. It is amazing how reading the Prophets, a verse or two jumps out and speaks about the future Messiah and his kingdom new covenant reign.

Rule No. 2

Interpreting Key Old Testament Words

Israel-Judah

One of the reasons people get confused when reading the Old Testament prophecies is because they apply an excessively literal understanding. If the prophetic words speak about 'Israel' or 'Judah', we think only in terms of the complete nation of Israel, or the ten tribes and for Judah - the two tribes. The problem is that after the Assyrian captivity of the ten northern tribes, this large majority of Israel, never returned to the promised land. They were assimilated into various cultures and lost forever. This has led to numerous spurious doctrines about modern day groups being the lost tribes. Instead of wasting time and useful brain energy in such matters, we need to see the prophecies where Israel is mentioned, which would be fulfilled in the new covenant when the Holy Spirit fell.

The Land

When we read of Israel being brought back and restored to the land, we must look to see the date of the prophecy. If a prophecy is speaking of Israel being restored to the land and it is from the time of the Babylonian captivity, then we know the ten tribes never returned. Therefore, we look for an interpretation, which makes sense from the viewpoint of the New Testament Apostles.

I will restore the fortunes of my people Israel. (Amos 9:14)

I will plant them on their land. (Amos 9:15)

After they finished speaking, James replied, "Brothers, listen to me. Simeon has related how God first visited the Gentiles, to take from them a people for his name. And with this the words of the prophets agree, just as it is written. (Acts 15:13-15)

As the presiding Apostle and Elder in Jerusalem, James makes the final decision in the discussion about whether Gentiles coming to Christ should keep the Mosaic Law or not. He uses the words of Amos 9 to prove that God is enlarging his people to include Gentiles and they are not obligated to keep the Law of Moses. Why would the Christian leaders think this might be the case? It is because these believing Gentiles were now part of Israel. They have been added in to the root of the olive tree. It was a reasonable question. I'm sure if another question were asked at the same time, a different answer would have been given. "Ok, James, Gentiles who have been added to Israel through belief in Jesus are exempt from the Law. I understand that, but what about the present Jews who are believers? Are they also free from the Mosaic law?" I cannot know what James would have said, but I have a strong conviction that it would have been something like, "Of course, we keep the Mosaic Law, we are Jews." It was not until later, when Apostle Paul began writing his letters, that the truth of the cross was fully understood; even Jews were free from the Mosaic Law. This was a radical message and Apostle Paul wrote plenty about this very issue. It was not until the fall of the year 70 AD, when Jerusalem and the Temple burned, that the whole Christian community knew that the old Laws were now obsolete.

James quoted only part of the prophecy in Amos. Yet, the passage in Amos is a continuous prophetic word ending with the promise of the land. We can also take from James' understanding that the prophetic word of Amos was not to be taken literally but applied to the new thing God was doing through Jesus. Thank God for Apostle Paul who takes the original land promise to Abraham and tells us what it now means for those under the new covenant.

For the promise to Abraham and his offspring that he would be heir of the world did not come through the law but through the righteousness of faith. (Romans 4:13)

Instead of identifying Abraham's original promise as the land of Palestine, notice how Paul changes it to the entire world. Under the new covenant a small promise becomes a much larger one. The whole world is now the 'holy land' and so the whole world is now our inheritance.

For students of the Bible, check out the *Bible Gate* and its translations. One of them has the English with the Greek below it. It is *Mounce Reverse - Interlinear New Testament.* As we can read, the word for the "land of promise" in Greek is 'kosmos.'

***For** gar **the** ho **promise** epangelia **that he** autos **would be** eimi **heir** klēronomos **of** kosmos **the world** kosmos **did not** ou **come to** ho **Abraham** Abraam **or** ē **to** ho **his** autos **descendants** sperma **through** dia **the law** nomos, ho **but** alla **through** dia **the righteousness** dikaiosynē **of faith** pistis.*

I also like the Message translation for this verse.

That famous promise God gave Abraham—that he and his children would possess the earth (The Message)

Jerusalem

When reading the Old Testament, we see passages where Jerusalem will be restored or be the light to the nations, how should we interpret these scriptures? Should we always seek the literal, depend on the context, or look for the Apostolic understanding? Apostle Paul, the author of Hebrews, help us on this point.

Tell me, you who desire to be under the law, do you not listen to the law? For it is written that Abraham had two sons, one by a slave woman and one by a free woman. But the son of the slave was born according to the flesh, while the son of the free woman was born through promise. Now this may be interpreted allegorically: these women are two covenants. One is from Mount Sinai, bearing children for slavery; she is Hagar. Now Hagar is Mount Sinai in Arabia; she corresponds to the present Jerusalem, for she is in slavery with her children. But the Jerusalem above is free, and she is our mother. (Galatians 4:21-25)

Apostle Paul lays down a principle of new covenant interpretation - Jerusalem of the new covenant is not the physical city but is to be understood in a spiritual sense. When we read from the book of Hebrews, it becomes clear – words mean different things, depending on which covenant is being addressed.

For you have not come to what may be touched, a blazing fire and darkness and gloom and a tempest and the sound of a trumpet and a voice whose words made the hearers beg that no further messages be spoken to them. For they could not endure the order that was given, "If even a beast touches the mountain, it shall be stoned." Indeed, so terrifying was the sight that Moses said, "I tremble with fear." But you have come to Mount Zion and to the city of the living God, the heavenly Jerusalem, and to innumerable angels in festal gathering, and to the assembly of the firstborn who are enrolled in heaven, and to God, the judge of all, and to the spirits of the righteous made perfect, and to Jesus, the mediator of a new covenant, and to the sprinkled blood that speaks a better word than the blood of Abel. (Hebrews 12:18-24)

To shorten this passage and get to its essence, we can say, "We have not come to Moses and the old covenant, but we have come to the new city of God, which is the new covenant people of God. And who made this all possible? It is Jesus, the mediator of the new covenant."

Law

When we read a restoration prophecy in the Old Testament there is often included a phrase about returning to and obeying the Laws of God. When applied to historic revivals within Israel and their returning to Jerusalem after captivity, we can be assured it is speaking of the Mosaic Law. This is the only Law they knew. A problem arises when we see words about a restored Law of God within prophetic passages, where Jesus and the new covenant times are clearly in view. The following passage in Jeremiah is a good example.

Behold, the days are coming, declares the LORD, when I will make a new covenant with the house of Israel and the house of Judah. (Jeremiah 31:31)

For this is the covenant that I will make with the house of Israel after those days, declares the LORD: I will put my law within them, and I will write it on their hearts. And I will be their God, and they shall be my people. (Jeremiah 31:33)

Later we will discuss in detail Jeremiah's new covenant prophecy but for now we are interested in the use of the words "My Law." If we were there at the time of Jeremiah and asked him, "What Law are you talking about, that will be part of this new covenant?" I think Jeremiah would have been puzzled by the question. There was only one law from God - the law of Moses. The difference is that under the old covenant these laws were written on stone and under the new covenant they would be written on the hearts of the people. Is that true?

When people embrace Jesus and are transferred into the kingdom, do they have an inward longing to observe the 613 Laws of Moses? Or are they filled with a new sense of love, peace and forgiveness? Therefore, when interpreting the words of Jeremiah concerning the Law of God, we must see it through a "Christocentric" understanding. The "Law of Christ" is the operative law of the new covenant, not the law of Moses.

Remnant

We know that after the Babylonian captivity only a few returned. The Bible often refers to this group as a *remnant*. Zechariah gives a prophecy about this remnant coming back and it has new covenant applications.

Thus says the LORD of hosts: I am jealous for Zion with great jealousy, and I am jealous for her with great wrath. Thus says the LORD: I have returned to Zion and will dwell in the midst of Jerusalem, and Jerusalem shall be called the faithful city, and the mountain of the LORD of hosts, the holy mountain. Thus says the LORD of hosts: Old men and old women shall again sit in the streets of Jerusalem, each with staff in hand because of great age. And the streets of the city shall be full of boys and girls playing in its streets. Thus says the LORD of hosts: If it is marvelous in the sight of the remnant of this people in those days, should it also be marvelous in my sight, declares the LORD of hosts? Thus says the LORD of hosts: Behold, I will save my people from the east country and from the west country, and I will bring them to dwell in the midst of Jerusalem. And they shall be my people, and I will be their God, in faithfulness and in righteousness." (Zechariah 8:2-6)

The prophet gives a word of encouragement to the remnant of returning captives. They are returning to Jerusalem, wanting a better life and the restoration of Israel to its former glory. God says he is with them and they shall live in peace and prosperity. Verse 12 says, *"And I will cause the remnant of this people to possess all these things."* The big question is, "Did they?" Did the post-exilic people of God experience life as the Prophet foretold? Not really. Life was difficult, they were generally poor, and they were not without enemies to stall or prevent their progress. Then, when Jerusalem was rebuilt, at least in part, and the temple finished, the old men wept because it was nothing compared to the former temple.

To fully grasp the meaning of these words of blessing we must see how the ultimate fulfillment was for the true remnant that Apostle Paul belonged to. *"So too, at the present time there is a remnant, chosen by grace."* The Apostle was addressing the difficult subject: Was God finished with Israel? He said that couldn't be true, because he himself was part of God's people, now by grace and not through the works of the law. The 'remnant' that received all these things were not the historic people who returned to Jerusalem 400 years before Jesus was born. Rather, they were the Jews of the first century, who embraced Jesus and entered the new covenant.

The Apostolic principle of interpreting these types of Old Testament passages gives us the true and final fulfillment.

With the change of covenants there is also a change in the meaning of words.

Rule No. 3

The Apostles' Interpretation is Our Example

There are many examples of an 'Apostolic Hermeneutic' found in the New Testament. When you read the Old Testament quotes, look to see if there is a new covenant interpretation.

In the second section we review 50 Old Testament passages, where a "Christocentric" and "Theological Interpretation" needs to be applied if we are to arrive at the full meaning of the passage.

Rule No. 4

Rely on the Holy Spirit

Without falling into a hole of personal subjectivism, we need the help of the Holy Spirit to rightly interpret the prophetic sections of the Old Testament.

The Apostles often quoted the Old Testament; and from the standpoint of the modern mind, they obviously did a poor job of it. One reason for the differences is they were quoting from the Septuagint version (Hebrew translated into Greek), whereas the Old Testament translation many use today is from a different version (probably from the Hebrew Masoretic text). Yet, we must admit there remain differences in what the Apostles quoted and the actual words in the Old Testament. We realize that the New Testament was written under the inspiration of the Holy Spirit and the words used by the Apostles were sufficient to convey the primary meaning for the new covenant purposes.

We have the same Holy Spirit that the Apostles did. No individual is the sole authority for interpreting Scripture, but we can pray and ask the Holy Spirit for assistance.

Rule No. 5

Look for the 'Christocentric Interpretation.'

The foundation for all God's truth is found in the person of Jesus. He clearly said that all the Law, the Prophets and the Psalms spoke of him. The Apostles spoke with authority and set the guidelines for what we would call, 'New Testament Theology.'

Here is a definition by Christopher Peppler: "The key contention is that scripture should be interpreted primarily from the perspective of Jesus' character, values, principles and priorities, as revealed directly or indirectly by the biblical revelation of what he said and did. This is called the 'Christocentric principle'.[48]

All of the Old Testament points to Jesus and his kingdom reign. When reading Scripture, it is necessary to look at how it relates to Jesus. The old covenant is no longer binding on Christians and has no authority; yet, we will study the Old Testament for centuries to come, so that we can obtain a greater revelation of Jesus and his glorious reign over the nations.

And beginning with Moses and all the Prophets, he interpreted to them in all the Scriptures the things concerning himself. (Luke 24:27)

Then he said to them, "These are my words that I spoke to you while I was still with you, that everything written about me in the Law of Moses and the Prophets and the Psalms must be fulfilled." Then he opened their minds to understand the Scriptures. (Luke 24:44-45)

---

[48] Christopher Peppler, The Christocentric Principle: A Jesus-Centered Herme-neutic, https://www.sats.edu.za/userfiles/Peppler,%20The%20Christocentric%20 Principle-A%20Jesus-Centred%20Hermeneutic.pdf

Since our goal is to 'understand the Scriptures', we need to follow the advice of Jesus and look at the Old Testament with 'Christo-centric' eyes.

Rule No. 6

Apply a "Theological Interpretation" to the Old Testament

We first look for how Jesus may be hidden in the words and meanings of Old Testament passages. Then, we also must apply the theology of the Apostles. This takes into consideration the major changes Jesus brought in with the new covenant. There are certain priorities which necessarily to apply in our interpretation of Scripture. Grace triumphs Law; love replaces wrath; forgiveness overcomes guilt; enemies are to be loved, not killed. The old covenant will never be re-instated. The new covenant is eternal. Applying the 'Theology of the Apostles' will greatly assist us in our study of the Bible. Coming to the central point - it is all about Jesus and the kingdom of God. Philip knew this, and it is the message he preached.

But when they believed Philip as he preached good news about the kingdom of God and the name of Jesus Christ, they were baptized, both men and women. (Acts 8:12)

Rule No. 7

Receive deeply of the 'fatness' of the Olive Tree

The Old Testament is a rich deposit of kingdom and new covenant revelation. Read, study and mediate upon these Scriptures. From its pages we are connected to our roots, the promises and prophecies given to old covenant Israel.

When we partake of the richness of the olive tree, we will receive a greater revelation of the kingdom. The church will focus on its mission, the nations will be discipled, and the Glory of God shall cover the earth. That my friends, is a life worth living!

Section Two
The Message of the Prophets

Exegetical and Hermeneutical
Analyses of 50 Old Testament Passages
in Connection to the Messianic Kingdom
and the Church

Introduction to Section Two

In this section we will examine individual prophetic passages which, in my opinion, are fulfilled in Christ and through his church. We are building on the foundation in the first section, using a Christocentric and Theological hermeneutic, applying the principle of a 'Corporate Christology' and using Paul's image of an olive tree to direct our exegesis.

From this point on there will be a single theme so chapter headings are no longer useful or needed. For easy reference each passage will follow the Old Testament order of books. There are hundreds of complete passages, verses and even parts of verses that make up this *'rich root'* for the church, but I have no interest or time to write a 5,000-page book. Hopefully others will be inspired and write about their insights, adding to what is presented here. Only the Prophets will be covered. This includes David (Peter called him a Prophet - Acts 2:30) and Daniel (Jewish tradition excludes Daniel among the Prophets, because his book is a written record of visions and not spoken prophecies.)

If it is true that the Old Testament Prophets spoke about the church and the age of the kingdom (even if they were not fully aware of what they were speaking), that would destroy the dispensational notion of the 'postponement' theory. It is the church that walks out the promises of the kingdom age. It also challenges us to recognize that there is a new covenant truth that we can extract from the Old Testament.

The passages which are quoted by New Testament authors are the easy ones. We already have their commentary and interpretation. What is more difficult but just as important are the many passages by the Prophets that are not quoted in the New Testament. These are the ones which get overlooked or ignored. Yet, within these numerous verses vital revelations concerning the kingdom of God can be found.

When reading the words of the Prophets we need to learn the language spoken. I'm not referring to their actual spoken language but to their covenantal language; the language used by the Prophets when speaking to Israel. When I read prophetic words in the Old Testament, I should not be swayed by literal language which only fits natural Israel. If we read of sacrifices and burnt offerings within a kingdom promise, we must see them through the theology of the New Testament. Jesus was the final offering. So, a theology based upon the finished work of Jesus is needed to understand the full meaning. By doing this we are reading what should be read into a passage. We need to see the truth behind the words that are written in the language of the old covenant.

When reading these passages, you will notice I prefer older commentaries. Not that there isn't any excellent modern scholarship - there is- but by using those scholars of previous generations, two things are accomplished. First, we gain insight into the church's biblical hermeneutic that which was used throughout most of church history. Second, we avoid the trouble of having to filter out dispensational interpretation, which applies an overly literal approach and loses the true meaning. As an example, according to the dispensationalists, *Israel* always means national or ethnic Israel, *mountains* always mean physical mountains, *Jerusalem* always means the actual city and so on.

With these guidelines we now turn to a selection of Old Testament promises which are part of the church's inheritance. These are promises for the age of the kingdom. In a single verse or passage there may be several promises. At times the passages speak less about a specific promise than they provide a picture, an image or a type, that reveal the kingdom of God. All these promises and various visions of the kingdom make up a foundation of truth that will guide us, encourage us and inject a passion in us for the advancing kingdom.

The Message of the Prophets

1. Psalms 2:1-8

Why do the nations rage
and the peoples plot in vain?
The kings of the earth set themselves,
and the rulers take counsel together,
against the LORD and against his Anointed, saying,
"Let us burst their bonds apart
and cast away their cords from us."
He who sits in the heavens laughs;
the Lord holds them in derision.
Then he will speak to them in his wrath,
and terrify them in his fury, saying,
"As for me, I have set my King on Zion, my holy hill."
I will tell of the decree:
The LORD said to me, "You are my Son;
today I have begotten you.
Ask of me, and I will make the nations your heritage,
and the ends of the earth your possession.

Psalm 2 is one of those passages where both the historical and future elements are present. If you read this shorty after it was written, it would have inspired you to believe that 'great things' were about to happen in your lifetime. It would have reinforced the knowledge that God's purpose would not be altered. It would have been read as referring to King David. It would have been a confirmation of God's will to defeat Israel's enemies. It would have meant that God was planning to make David not only King of Israel, but over the whole world as well.

During my years of ministry, I have come across people with numerous different conspiracy theories about who is ruling the world. I've learned that arguing with them is of little use. My standard answer is, "Yes, there are evil people and evil associations of people, that are working against God's will on the earth, but it is important to remember - their influence is only temporary." I will not spend any mental or emotional energy on such speculations. The kingship of Jesus will continue to increase over all his enemies. This is my focus.

What does the Psalmist say about God's reaction to evil men and their intentions? *"He who sits in the heavens laughs (Ps. 2:4)."*

If you had lived several hundred years after David died, this passage would have taken on a very different interpretation. David and his son Solomon achieved wonderful things; but he never became King of the world, nor did his son. During the days of Isaiah, Jeremiah and Ezekiel, David was still the focus and the hope of Israel. His name evoked the hope that Israel would be restored to its former glory. Remembering David brought back the positive memories of Israel's 'good old days' and provided dreams of a better future, a future when a person like David would return and make Israel great again.

As we move into the first century, a new king like David had come. Jesus gave the old promises of a king a different look. A fresh interpretation was needed. After Jesus finished his work and ascended into heaven, the Apostles saw Psalm 2 in an even fuller dimension. Jesus reigned from David's throne, but it was a heavenly, not an earthly throne.

Psalm 2 was a significant passage for the new covenant Apostles. Most of the chapter - around 60% - is quoted throughout the New Testament. Why? The most important thing during the first century – as well as today - is that God has made Jesus both Lord and Christ (Acts 2:36).

Acts 4:25-26

Who by the mouth of our father David, your servant, said by the Holy Spirit,
" 'Why did the Gentiles rage,
and the peoples plot in vain?

The kings of the earth set themselves,
and the rulers were gathered together,
against the Lord and against his Anointed."

We are not to be fearful. God has installed his king, and everything will be ok. Jesus is king of the world and possesses all authority in heaven and on earth. I love how the Psalm describes God as *'laughing'* at the threats of the heathen. Since God is assuring us his Son will be victorious and we are in 'The Messiah,' our victory is also sure.

God has set his Son upon the throne and has given him the kingdom. We are called to hope and not despair.

Another passage in the book of Acts, which refers to Psalm 2, is found in chapter 13. Paul and his companions were in Antioch (Pisidia) and were speaking in the synagogue. Paul drew their attention to the history of Israel and then to their current time, when God had sent them a Savior; Jesus. His death was not final; God raised him from the dead. Then Paul makes an amazing statement - his apostolic interpretation of Psalm 2.

Acts 13:32-34

And we bring you the good news that what God promised to the
fathers, this he has fulfilled to us their children by raising Jesus, as
also it is written in Psalm 2,
" 'You are my Son,
today I have begotten you.'
And as for the fact that he raised him from the dead, no more to
return to corruption, he has spoken in this way,
" 'I will give you the holy and sure blessings of David.'

See how Apostle Paul links Psalm 2 with the 'Good News' of the kingdom. Because God has *"set my King on Zion"* now, *"I will make the nations your heritage, and the ends of the earth your possession."*

At his Ascension, Jesus was established king over the nations. The ongoing work of the church is to proclaim this message to the nations and bring them under his authority. Jesus is the center of everything God is doing. He is the administrator of his purposes. The message of Psalm 2 continues today. This is Christocentric; this is the Apostolic Hermeneutic.

Are we asking for Nations?

2. Psalm 22:27-28

All the ends of the earth shall remember
and turn to the LORD,
and all the families of the nations
shall worship before you.
For kingship belongs to the LORD,
and he rules over the nations.

Many prophetic words have explicit references, or at least allude to the covenants with Abraham and David. These two covenants make up the foundation for a majority of the kingdom promises. Abraham and David are never forgotten. God made promises to these men and He intended to keep them.

Today, as we proclaim the goodness of God, we expect people from the '*ends of the earth*' to remember and turn to Jesus.

What I find intriguing about many of the Old Testament prophetic passages is that they are quite clear about God's intention to go beyond the borders of Israel. The families or nations of the world are promised to Abraham and yet, when Jesus came to the people of Israel, they were not interested in any nation beyond themselves. A better reading of their own Scriptures would have prepared them.

The renowned nineteenth century preacher of London, Charles Spurgeon, made a comment worth considering:

"In readying this verse one is struck with the Messiah's missionary spirit. It is evidently his grand consolation that Jehovah will be known throughout all places of his dominion. All the ends of the world shall remember and turn unto the Lord. Out from the inner circle of the present church the blessing is to spread in growing power until the remotest parts of the earth shall be ashamed of their idols, mindful of the true God, penitent for their offences, and unanimously earnest for reconciliation with Jehovah. Then shall false worship cease, and all the kindreds of the nations shall worship before thee, O thou only living and true God."[49]

I love Spurgeon's phrase, "Then shall false worship cease." This is our vision for the kingdom. This is the Prophets of old spurring us onward. This is the dream of God for the church.

In Hebrew, the phrase *"kingship belongs to the Lord"* would read *'kingship belongs to Yahweh.'* True kingship went beyond David; it was the exclusive domain of Yahweh. When Jesus came, there was a process whereby this kingship was to be transferred to the Son. All authority in heaven and earth was to come to the Son (Matthew 28:18). By the death and resurrection of Jesus, he received the kingship that had once been held by the Father. Today, it is to the name of 'Jesus' that every knee will bow. It is Jesus who transforms the nations. This is the good news. This is the gospel.

In modern preaching, the gospel is an invitation to receive Jesus. The concept of an *'invitation'* can be found in the New Testament; yet, the Old Testament background for the good news presents itself in the form of an *'announcement'*, more than an invitation (Isaiah 52:7). Preaching the gospel is the announcement that God has made Jesus king of the world and his kingdom is now in session. Our response is to gladly receive the forgiveness of sins and submit to the king.

This passage alludes to both the Abrahamic and the Davidic covenants. Both *'all the families'* and *'kingship'* are mentioned here. Jesus came to open the door for all the families of the earth, so that they could enjoy being under his reign. His kingship and reign continue through the church.

Abraham and David are the foundation upon which the kingdom is proclaimed.

---

[49] Charles Spurgeon, The Treasury of David, Kregel Academic, 2004

The mission of the church will not be complete until all nations worship King Jesus.

3. Psalm 45:6

Your throne, O God, is forever and ever.
The scepter of your kingdom is a scepter of uprightness.

This seems to be a straightforward Messianic prophecy. The strength of this interpretation comes from its usage in the book of Hebrews, *"But of the Son he says, "Your throne, O God, is forever and ever, the scepter of uprightness is the scepter of your kingdom (Hebrews 1:8).*

Albert Barnes, a nineteenth century American theologian and pastor, known best for his 14 volume Bible commentary published in the 1830's, takes the following approach:

"Thy throne, O God, is forever and ever - This passage is quoted by the author of the Epistle to the Hebrews in proof that the Messiah is exalted above the angels, and it is, beyond all question, adduced by him as having original reference to the Messiah."[50]

The passage also declares that the kingdom is a righteous rule. The reign of Jesus brings justice to the nations. When we demonstrate the righteousness of Christ, we advance the kingdom of God and it flows out to the nations.

Cambridge Bible for Schools and Colleges takes a more exegetical approach and it states a different possible interpretation:

"The older expositors, who regarded the Psalm as directly Messianic, of course felt no difficulty, and saw in the words a recognition of the Deity of Christ. But the tone and contents of the Psalm make it clear that it is addressed to some actual king. Could such a king be so addressed? It is argued that judges were called *gods* (Exodus 21:6; Exodus 22:8-9; Exodus 22:28(?); 1 Samuel

---

[50] Albert Barnes, Barnes Notes on the Old and New Testaments, Baker Books, 19th edition, 1983

2:25); that the theocratic king as the representative of God was said to sit "on the throne of Jehovah" (1 Chronicles 28:5; 1 Chronicles 29:23); that a prophet can predict that the house of David should be *as God* (Zechariah 12:8); that *Elohim* is applied to men in the sense of divine or supernatural (Exodus 7:1; 1 Samuel 28:13)."[51]

Even though it is likely that those who read Isaiah in the centuries preceding the Messiah may have read this as referring to an actual king, I draw my conclusion from the apostolic interpretation in the book of Hebrews. Nevertheless, we must recognize that, as God's covenant people (both old and new covenant), we are called to be "kings" and in a lesser sense - "gods."

Righteousness is the mark of the Kingdom.

4. Psalm 48:1-2

Great is the LORD and greatly to be praised
in the city of our God!
His holy mountain, beautiful in elevation,
is the joy of all the earth,
Mount Zion, in the far north,
the city of the great King.

Mount Zion transcends from a physical mountain in the Old Testament, to the church in the New Testament. We are Mount Zion (Hebrews 12:22). The church should be filled with exuberant praise to our king. Worship is a vital part of our kingdom advancing calling. If we force a literal interpretation, we end up celebrating around a physical mountain. Once we apply a simple Apostolic Hermeneutic, we see the beauty of the poem. God is praised in the new Jerusalem - the *Mount Zion* of the new covenant.

The church is the home of King Jesus. We dance around in his presence. We rejoice over his goodness. He is the joy, not only of the church, but of the whole earth. They need to know it.

---

[51] George Gillanders Findlay, Cambridge Bible for Schools and Colleges, Forgotten Books, 2017

The Church is the City of our Great King.

5. Psalm 72:8-9, 17-20

May he have dominion from sea to sea,
and from the River to the ends of the earth!
May desert tribes bow down before him,
and his enemies lick the dust!
May his name endure forever,
his fame continue as long as the sun!
May people be blessed in him,
all nations call him blessed!
Blessed be the LORD, *the God of Israel,*
who alone does wondrous things.
Blessed be his glorious name forever;
may the whole earth be filled with his glory!
Amen and Amen!
The prayers of David, the son of Jesse, are ended.

David was nearing the end of his life when he wrote a Psalm for his son - Solomon. The message was simple - Israel should not lose hope; because Solomon would fulfill what God had promised. Once again, the interpretation changes, depending on when you were born. If you were alive during the reign of Solomon, you would apply this passage to the wonderful blessings enjoyed under his rule and hope for greater things. If you were born during the days of Jeremiah, you would interpret this to say that someday in the future God would raise up a Messiah who would be like 'King David.' Today we understand that these words went beyond what God had planned for Solomon and spoke of the reign of Christ.

We live in this glorious time of the kingdom of God. Jesus began to fulfill this promise at his ascension. He continues to fulfill it through the church. The church is God's people, through whom he fills the earth with his manifest glory. Our joy is taking this glory to all the nations. To a people without hope. To a people who no longer dream. Are you willing to share God's glory with the nations?

The Mission of the Church is to share God's Glory with all Nations.

6. Psalm 89:3-4, 14, 27-29

You have said, "I have made a covenant with my chosen one;
I have sworn to David my servant:
'I will establish your offspring forever,
and build your throne for all generations.'" Selah
Righteousness and justice are the foundation of your throne;
steadfast love and faithfulness go before you.
And I will make him the firstborn,
the highest of the kings of the earth.
My steadfast love I will keep for him forever,
and my covenant will stand firm for him.
I will establish his offspring forever
and his throne as the days of the heavens.

Once again, David is spoken of and he represents what the future 'David' will accomplish. We learned earlier about 'righteousness' and how it is foundational to God's throne; now 'justice' is added. The church is the voice of justice on the earth, or at least it should be. We are a friend of the downtrodden, the outcast, and those who have seldom experienced justice. We need people who are committed to applying 'Godly justice' to institutions which are corrupt. The people of the kingdom need to realize that they are not just called to 'proclaim' the good news of Jesus, but must also see that it is applied in all cultural institutions.

God reminds us that his covenant with David is not a temporal covenant; it will continue to exist. As long as heaven exists, the covenant with David continues. Jesus is the highest King, he is and always will be!

The Mission of the Church is to bring Justice to the Nations.

7. Psalm 89:3

You have said, "I have made a covenant with my chosen one;
I have sworn to David my servant:
'I will establish your offspring forever,
and build your throne for all generations.'

This is another promise made to David, which makes up what we know as the 'Davidic Covenant.' I covered the dispensational approach in my book "*Glorious Kingdom*" and will not repeat it here. Simply put, they say that the Davidic Covenant is for the future millennial kingdom. Does Jesus fulfill this word? Of course, he does. Because of his willingness to go to the cross, he ascended and at his enthronement he was given the kingdom (Philippians 2:5-11, Daniel 7:13-14). He now reigns as King. Does this prophecy continue to be fulfilled in and through the church? Yes, it does. "*For all generations*" does not mean that the fulfillment ended in the first century. The Messiah and his kingdom cannot be separated from his body; the church.

Since we have a Glorious Kingdom, we also need a Glorious Church.

8. Psalm 122

I was glad when they said to me,
"Let us go to the house of the LORD!"
Our feet have been standing
within your gates, O Jerusalem!
Jerusalem—built as a city
that is bound firmly together,
to which the tribes go up,
the tribes of the LORD,
as was decreed for Israel,
to give thanks to the name of the LORD.
There thrones for judgment were set,
the thrones of the house of David.
Pray for the peace of Jerusalem!

"May they be secure who love you!
Peace be within your walls
and security within your towers!"
For my brothers and companions' sake
I will say, "Peace be within you!"
For the sake of the house of the LORD our God,
I will seek your good.

There have been few phrases that have tugged at the hearts of millions like when the psalmist wrote, *"Pray for the peace of Jerusalem."* It reminds us of recent and historical conflicts within Israel. It carries with it a sadness from knowing that 'peace' is not a word we can use to describe present day Jerusalem.

As in any Scriptural passage, context is where we begin our exegesis. The first thing to note is that this psalm is included as a *"Song of Ascents."* As the people walked to their place of worship, they sang these songs to each other. This was before the temple was built and during the reign of David. We know that when David brought back the Ark of the Covenant, he did not return it to the 'tent of worship' with its Mosaic Laws of worship, but he 'pitched a tent' in the city of David and placed the Ark there.

Albert Barnes provides insight into this psalm of David:

"Pray for the peace of Jerusalem - This is the language, which those who were going up to the city - to the house of the Lord - addressed to each other, expressing the joyful feelings of their hearts at their own near approach to the city. It breathes the desire that all would pray for the peace and prosperity of a city so dear to their own souls; where the worship of God was celebrated; where God himself dwelt; where justice was administered: a city of so much importance and so much influence in the land. To us now it inculcates the duty of praying for the church: its peace; its unity; its prosperity; its increase; its influence on our country and on the world at large. It is a prayer that the church may not be divided by schism or heresy; that its members may cherish for each other right feelings; that there may be no jealousies, no envyings, and no jars; that the different branches of the church may regard and treat each other with kindness, with respect, and with mutual recognition; that prosperity may attend them all."[52]

Barnes' words of prayer for the church need to be repeated in every local gathering of saints. Are we praying for the church?

John Gill, who preached in the church of Charles Spurgeon - 100 years before him - wrote one of the first and largest commentaries of the Old and New Testament. His comments on verse 3 provide theological insight to the common practice of interpreting these types of Old Testament passages:

"In David's time, the upper and lower city were joined together, the streets regularly built, houses contiguous, not straggling about, here and there... So the church of God, like that, is built in a good situation, on a rock and hill, where it is firm and visible; like a city full of inhabitants, governed by wholesome laws, under proper officers; a free city, which enjoys many privileges and immunities; a well-fortified one, having salvation for walls and bulwarks about it; a royal city, the city of the great King, the city of our God"[53]

I find it interesting that both Barnes and Gill make a smooth transition, from the historical context of Jerusalem, to the church. There are no long debates on why we should read this Old Testament psalm with a new covenant understanding. This was the accepted method of reading Old Testament Scripture before the time of 'dispensationalism.' Dispensationalists insist on a 'literal' interpretation and an absolute separation between Israel and the church. Today, many churches have 'dispensational' leanings, so no easy transition to the church would likely be heard. It would be interpreted to apply only to 'present Jerusalem' and the need for peace.

---

[52] Albert Barnes, Notes on the Bible by Albert Barnes [1834], Text Courtesy of Internet Sacred Texts Archive, Bible Hub

[53] John Gill, Gill's Commentary and Exposition of the Old and New Testaments, Baker Book House, 1980

Pray for the Peace of the New Jerusalem.

The Prophet Isaiah

We have little biblical knowledge of Isaiah as a person. It is likely he was related to royalty because of his relationships with the kings of his day and because he was knowledgeable of world affairs. He begins his book by saying his visions were in the days of Uzziah, Jotham, Ahaz and Hezekiah (Isaiah 1:1). In the sixth chapter, Isaiah had a vision of God's throne, which occurred "*in the year Hezekiah died*" (Isaiah 6:1). Tradition has Isaiah being 'sawn asunder' by Manasseh. With these dates in place, we can place the time of Isaiah's ministry from 739 B.C. to 690 B.C.

Isaiah lived approximately 700 years before the arrival of Jesus. The predictive prophecies of Isaiah are so accurate, that critics attempt to create a second Isaiah (who wrote chapters 40-66), or that the entire book was written during the Babylonian period. If the early dates are correct, then he made prophecies 150 years before their fulfillment. He even named the Persian King, Cyrus. Since we have Prophets, which speak for God, we should not have problems with their supernatural ability to see events in the future.

The book of Isaiah is large, covering complex issues and containing numerous theological issues worthy of study. However, our intent is to show 'kingdom promises for the kingdom age.' Therefore, we will limit our study to a few chapters and passages which best reveal Jesus and his kingdom of the covenant.

9. Isaiah 11:1

There shall come forth a shoot from the stump of Jesse,
and a branch from his roots shall bear fruit.

We move now several hundred years from the time of King David to the ministry of Isaiah. David is not mentioned in this verse, but his father Jesse becomes a representative of David. This is a Messianic prophecy about Jesus being the branch, which comes from the root of Jesse (David). When Paul wrote about the Olive tree and its '*rich root*', the covenant with David was included. In Jeremiah 23:5 we have the same promise:

Behold, the days are coming, declares the LORD, when I will raise up for David a righteous Branch, and he shall reign as king and deal wisely, and shall execute justice and righteousness in the land.

Ezekiel 37:24 also claims a new David is coming:

My servant David shall be king over them, and they shall all have one shepherd. They shall walk in my rules and be careful to obey my statutes.

God has chosen his Son and is completely satisfied that He will defeat all his enemies and take possession of the nations. Those who are '*In Christ*' are joint-heirs with him and therefore engaged in the defeat of his enemies. The nations of the world will progressively come under the Lordship of Christ.

The Davidic Covenant is being fulfilled by King Jesus, as he rules over his people - the church - and the nations. Jesus fulfills the prophecy in his ascension. Yet, the whole point of being King is to rule and that is what's happening now as the church, under the authority of their king, subdues nations.

Isaiah is certainly a Prophet of the Kingdom. His book is part of what is called "The Major Prophets" only because of the size of the book. There are more New Testament quotes from the book of Isaiah than any other. He sees the coming of the Messiah, his suffering and his kingship. He describes the age of the kingdom and the glories of God's eternal covenant.

Roots are to Produce Fruit.

10. Isaiah 9:1-2

But there will be no gloom for her who was in anguish. In the former time he brought into contempt the land of Zebulun and the land of Naphtali, but in the latter time he has made glorious the way of the sea, the land beyond the Jordan, Galilee of the nations. The people

who walked in darkness have seen a great light; those who dwelt in
a land of deep darkness, on them has light shone.

Alexander MacLaren (1810-1910) was a Baptist minister at Union Chapel in Manchester, England, for 45 years. He wrote beautifully about the background and future implications of this verse:

"The darker the cloud, the brighter is the rainbow. This prophecy has for its historical background the calamitous reign of the weak and wicked Ahaz, during which the heart of the nation was bowed, like a forest before the blast, by the dread of foreign invasion and conquest. The prophet predicts a day of gloom and anguish, and then, out of the midst of his threatening's, bursts this glorious vision, sudden as sunrise. With consummate poetic art, the consequences of Messiah's rule are set forth before He Himself is brought into view."[54]

Barnes gives us the historical perspective and the prophetic significance of this verse:

"The immediate connection seems to require us to understand it of deliverance from the calamities that were impending over the nation then. They would be afflicted, but they would be delivered. The tribes of Israel would be carried captive away; and Judah would also be removed. This calamity would particularly affect the ten tribes of Israel - the northern part of the land, the regions of Galilee - "for those tribes would be carried away not to return." Yet this region also would be favored with an especially striking manifestation of light. I see no reason to doubt that the language of the prophet here is adapted to extend into that future period when the Messiah should come to that dark region and become both its light and its deliverer. Isaiah may have referred to the immediate deliverance of the nation from impending calamities, but there is a fullness and richness of the language that seems to be

---

[54] Alexander MacLaren, MacLaren Expositions of Holy Scripture,

applicable only to the Messiah. So, it is evidently understood in Matthew 4:13-16."[55]

The prophetic element is certainly included, because Matthew includes these words from Isaiah.

Matthew 4:13-17

And leaving Nazareth he went and lived in Capernaum by the sea, in the territory of Zebulun and Naphtali, so that what was spoken by the prophet Isaiah might be fulfilled:
"The land of Zebulun and the land of Naphtali,
the way of the sea, beyond the Jordan, Galilee of the Gentiles—
the people dwelling in darkness
have seen a great light,
and for those dwelling in the region and shadow of death,
on them a light has dawned."
From that time Jesus began to preach, saying, "Repent, for the kingdom of heaven is at hand."

The place, known previously as a land of darkness, now has a '*great light.*' The connection with King Jesus and his reign is noted by Matthew, as he finishes this section with Jesus preaching that the kingdom was at hand. We have in this verse a prophecy of about what will happen in the '*last days.*' The Messiah came and established his kingdom in the final days of the old covenant.

Isaiah 9:6-7

For to us a child is born,
to us a son is given;
and the government shall be upon his shoulder,
and his name shall be called
Wonderful Counselor, Mighty God,
Everlasting Father, Prince of Peace.
Of the increase of his government and of peace

---

[55] Albert Barnes, Notes on the Bible by Albert Barnes [1834], Text Courtesy of Internet Sacred Texts Archive, Bible Hub

there will be no end,
on the throne of David and over his kingdom,
to establish it and to uphold it
with justice and with righteousness
from this time forth and forevermore.
The zeal of the LORD of hosts will do this.

This prophetic word for the future day of the Messiah's reign can be used as a test case for a 'Christocentric' interpretation. Every Christmas season we hear Isaiah quoted and gladly receive the promise of the Son of God coming to earth. Yet, because of their theology, many separate the *"Child is born"* from *"The increase of his government."* The former is the incarnation, whereas the words about government are to be fulfilled only in the future millennium. There is nothing in the text that should lead to this understanding. Only when theological presumptions (dispensationalism) are forced into the text would anyone separate verse six from verse seven by centuries of time.

Will the reign of King Jesus continue to increase? Yes, it will. Isaiah prophesied it. The kingdom will be enlarged today and in the future. Nation after nation will see spiritual transformation. How will this be accomplished? By the people of the kingdom - the church.

Luke 4:43

"But he said to them, "I must preach the good news of the kingdom of God to the other towns as well; for I was sent for this purpose. "

Jesus was sent to earth for a single purpose. Was it to die for our sins? Yes, he came and went to the cross for the forgiveness of sins, yet the cross of Jesus was about bringing people into the kingdom. That was the goal. Since the kingdom of God was spiritual rather than a military conquest, a rebirth from heaven was necessary to enter the kingdom (John 3:3). Jesus came to bring God's kingdom to earth. The gospel is 'Good News." The kingdom has come! Jesus and his kingdom are our message. This is what Philip taught.

Acts 8:12

But when they believed Philip as he preached good news about the kingdom of God and the name of Jesus Christ, they were baptized, both men and women.

If we ignore this prophecy from Isaiah along with multitudes of others, we will do great harm to the full and rich revelation of the kingdom of God. A reading of these prophecies must include the church; otherwise we lose them or postpone them to the future and both are unacceptable. Jesus came to earth with a central message - the arrival of God's Kingdom to earth. The Great Light has Come.

The Reign of Jesus is in session. It is advancing. And its increase will have no end. This is good news.

11. Isaiah 27:6

In days to come Jacob shall take root,
Israel shall blossom and put forth shoots
and fill the whole world with fruit.

This is one of my favorite verses from Isaiah. I am confounded that many miss what should be obvious. This is not about modern Israel filling the world with avocados and mangoes. Much of Scripture is about God desiring his people to be fruitful. When Jesus came, he found Israel as a fruitless nation and this was the key reason they lost the kingdom (Matthew 21:43). The church is called to be a fruitful nation that fills the world with the goodness of God.

A passage like this requires us to understand how the New Testament authors viewed the dramatic changes that occurred with the death and resurrection of Jesus. The kingdom of God is not winning a military battle; it is experiencing a spiritual transformation. We are not looking for natural fruit, but spiritual. We are looking for patience, kindness, faithfulness, justice, grace and love.

"In days to come" is a reference to the coming of the Messiah. Between Isaiah's time and the first century, there were no great days

in which Israel influenced the world. Why does Isaiah mention Jacob? It was common for the Old Testament Prophets to use one of the Patriarchs of Israel when speaking of the whole nation. The true faith of Israel begins with the God of Abraham, Isaac and Jacob. From Jacob came the twelve tribes of Israel (Jacob's name was changed to Israel). Who will receive the promises God gave Abraham? Apostle Paul writes, *"And if you are Christ's, then you are Abraham's offspring, heirs according to promise (Galatians 3:29)*. No one is stealing Israel's promises. When a Gentile comes to Christ, they are made part of the family of Abraham. That's the true Abrahamic faith, which comes through their Messiah.

Gill states plainly (and correctly) that we have a passage here which is fulfilled in the church:

"That is, the posterity of Jacob, the seed of Israel, in a spiritual sense; such who are Israelites indeed, in whom there is no guile; these shall be so far from being plucked up, or rooted out of the vineyard, the church, that they shall take deeper root, and their roots shall spread yet more and more; they shall be rooted and grounded in the love of God, and also in Christ, and be built up in him, as well as firmly settled and established in the church."[56]

I love what Gill says about the church, "Their roots shall spread yet more and more." The church is not finished; we may be only at the beginning. The growth of the church is the expansion of the kingdom. The spread of the God's love to the world is God's kingdom in its transformational power.

God's Kingdom people are called to fill the world with the Fruit of the Holy Spirit.

12. Isaiah 42:1-4

Behold my servant, whom I uphold,
my chosen, in whom my soul delights;

---

[56] John Gill, Gill's Commentary and Exposition of the Old and New Testaments, Baker Book House, 1980

I have put my Spirit upon him;
he will bring forth justice to the nations.
He will not cry aloud or lift up his voice,
or make it heard in the street;
a bruised reed he will not break,
and a faintly burning wick he will not quench;
he will faithfully bring forth justice.
He will not grow faint or be discouraged
till he has established justice in the earth;
and the coastlands wait for his law.

The passages about the "*servant*" are widely accepted by biblical scholars as Messianic. Where students of Scripture differ is in the timing of the work of the Messiah in bringing "*justice to the nations.*" Whenever Old Testament passages speak of the Messiah and his work among the nations, dispensationalists separate his 'kingdom' activity from his 'saving' work. They teach his first coming did not establish the kingdom of God, but it was postponed until he returns a second time.

There is nothing in the words of Isaiah, that would cause us to separate his '*receiving the Spirit*' from his work of bringing '*justice to the nations.*' One leads to the other. We make a mistake when we lose sight of the mission of the church, which carries on the ministry of Jesus in the earth. With King Jesus guiding us, the *church will bring justice to the nations.*

What is the meaning of the final line that speaks of the law of the Messiah? The question we need to ask is, "What law?" It is not the 'Law of Moses" that will transform the nations - it is the Law of Christ. His Law - that is what we need.

Justice in the Nations is accomplished by the Spirit and Through the Church.

13. Isaiah 49:5-6

And now the LORD says,
he who formed me from the womb to be his servant,

to bring Jacob back to him;
and that Israel might be gathered to him—
for I am honored in the eyes of the LORD,
and my God has become my strength—
he says:
"It is too light a thing that you should be my servant
to raise up the tribes of Jacob
and to bring back the preserved of Israel;
I will make you as a light for the nations,
that my salvation may reach to the end of the earth.

First, this passage is about the restoration of Israel. Second, before we can see the prophetic significance from a present kingdom point of view, we need to understand how these types of 'restoration prophecies' are interpreted by the Apostles of the New Testament. Should we be expecting national Israel to be restored to Old Covenant status and be the people who are 'now' the light to the nations? This would be the view of dispensationalists. The New Testament takes a different point of view. The New Testament authors see 'restoration' passages as being fulfilled in the coming of Jesus, the coming of his kingdom and the establishment of the new covenant. The Apostles used their theology, taught to them by Jesus and now revealed through the Holy Spirit, to determine the meaning of these types of passages.

It is the church that is the light to the nations. It is the church that will take the goods news of salvation to the world. The church fulfills this prophecy.

We need a different word than *'fulfilled.'* Especially since we tend to define it as coming to its logical end. If we see prophecies of the Old Testament as stopping and having no significance for the church, we are being robbed. We are giving up our inheritance that has been given to us by Jesus.

Since Christ fulfills all Old Testament promises, we can say with confidence - so does the church. He is the head of the church and we are his body. Have we forgotten this? Jesus died on the cross to defeat sin, Satan, and death; to deliver us out of darkness and to offer us the forgiveness of sin. Why? So, we can walk in the kingdom. So, we can walk in everything the Scriptures promise and this includes those kingdom promises in the Old Testament.

We cannot fully interpret these Old Testament prophetic verses separate from the coming of Jesus and the new covenant. Passages like this and others become the '*root*' of the church.

Who are these people, that bring salvation to the nations? It is the church. This is our promise. This is part of being grafted into the rich root of Israel.

14. Isaiah 51:4

Give attention to me, my people,
and give ear to me, my nation;
for a law will go out from me,
and I will set my justice for a light to the peoples.

For this verse we have an interpretation by an early church father; Justin Martyr. He was a second-century philosopher who studied the works of the Stoics, Aristotelians, Pythagoreans, and Platonists. One day while on a walk, he met an old man who told him about the Prophets and how they spoke of the coming Messiah. Justin was shortly converted to Christ and became one of Christianity's early apologists. We have a written account of his debate with Trypho, who was a committed Jew. Justin explains the difference between the old and the new covenants. He says that with the coming of Christ the old is no longer valid. The whole debate is how the words of the Old Testament Prophets bear witness to Christ and his activity in creating a new people by the Holy Spirit:

"There will be no other God, O Trypho, nor was there from eternity any other existing" (I thus addressed him) …But we do not trust through Moses or through the law; for then we would do the same as yourselves. But now--(for I have read that there shall be a final law, and a covenant, the chiefest of all, which it is now incumbent on all men to observe, as many as are seeking after the inheritance of God. For the law promulgated on Horeb is now old and belongs to yourselves alone; but *this* is for all universally. Now, law placed against law has abrogated that which is before it, and a covenant which comes after in like manner has put an end to the previous one; and an eternal and final law--namely, Christ--has been given to us, and the covenant is trustworthy, after which there shall be no law, no commandment, no ordinance. Have you not read this which Isaiah says: 'Hearken unto Me, hearken unto Me, my people; and, ye kings, give ear unto Me: for a law shall go forth from Me, and My judgment shall be for a light to the nations. My righteousness approaches swiftly, and My salvation shall go forth, and nations shall trust in Mine arm?'[57]

How did the early church fathers interpret the Old Testament Prophets? Here is an excellent example. Justin Martyr quotes Isaiah about a 'law' going forth and gives it a Christocentric interpretation. He says the final law is Christ. He says the present covenant has "put an end" to the previous one. What we see here is not a literal understanding of Isaiah's words, but he is reading these ancient words in view of the new covenant.

The Church is under God's Law - the Law of Christ.

15. Isaiah 54

In this chapter we have an excellent example of new covenant truth spoken by a Prophet, living under the old covenant.

54:1

Sing, O barren one, who did not bear;
break forth into singing and cry aloud,
you who have not been in labor!
For the children of the desolate one will be more
than the children of her who is married," says the LORD.

---

[57] Justin Martyr, Dialogue with Trypho, Ante-Nicene Fathers, Vol. I

Who does the Prophet refer to in the symbolism of these two women? One is called *"married"* and the other - *"barren one?"* We are fortunate to have a New Testament commentary on this passage. In the book of Galatians, Apostle Paul uses the words of Isaiah to make his point about the old and new covenant.

Galatians 4:21-27

Tell me, you who want to be under the law, are you not aware of what the law says? For it is written that Abraham had two sons, one by the slave woman and the other by the free woman. His son by the slave woman was born according to the flesh, but his son by the free woman was born as the result of a divine promise. These things are being taken figuratively: The women represent two covenants. One covenant is from Mount Sinai and bears children who are to be slaves: This is Hagar. Now Hagar stands for Mount Sinai in Arabia and corresponds to the present city of Jerusalem, because she is in slavery with her children. But the Jerusalem that is above is free, and she is our mother. For it is written:

"Be glad, barren woman,
you who never bore a child;
shout for joy and cry aloud,
you who were never in labor;
because more are the children of the desolate woman
than of her who has a husband."

Galatians 4:30-31

But what does the Scripture say? "Cast out the slave woman and her son, for the son of the slave woman shall not inherit with the son of the free woman." So, brothers, we are not children of the slave but of the free woman.

How should we understand this? I think it is clear. Those, who insist on remaining in the old covenant, will not inherit the promises of God. This is a serious blow to those who insist that only natural Israel can inherit the Old Testament promises. No, it is the people of the free woman, of the heavenly Jerusalem, of the new covenant, that are the people of God and they will inherit what God has promised.

We have an excellent example of what can be called a 'Christo-centric' interpretation in this passage from Paul's letter to the Galatians. Paul reads the Old Testament from the position of the coming of Christ and the establishment of the new covenant. Paul realized that the old covenant and the people clinging to it were replaced by the new covenant and the people embracing it. If Apostle Paul were alive today and preaching this message, he would be accused of teaching 'replacement theology.' I think he would object to the term - as I and many others do - as he said, I was *"circumcised on the eighth day, of the people of Israel, of the tribe of Benjamin, a Hebrew of Hebrews; as to the law, a Pharisee; as to zeal, a persecutor of the church; as to righteousness under the law, blameless* (Philippians 3:5-6). This goes to the heart of Paul's argument in Romans 11. How can Israel be rejected, when he himself and the other Jews were included in the new covenant?

Paul is in the middle of a discussion about the Law of Moses and the advantages of the new covenant. He reminds his readers of the two sons of Abraham. The first son was of the '*flesh*', born from a slave. He did not fulfill the promise given to Abraham. The second son, born of the '*free woman*', was the fulfillment. Then Paul tells us, that these two women - one slave and one free - when taken 'figuratively', are the two covenants. Paul does what he often does in making a theological argument - quotes a passage in the Old Testament as 'proof' of what he is writing.

The woman in Isaiah, who was never in labor, now is the one who has more children. She represents the nations - the Gentiles under the new covenant. In the future, from Isaiah's perspective, Gentiles would far outnumber Jewish believers. The new covenant, born out of a promise to Abraham is far more superior than the old covenant. Therefore, the expectation of Israel, which over time became 'Jewish eschatology', had to be enlarged so that it could incorporate Gentiles. We are not sure if all this was in the mind of Isaiah while writing it. Things can be spoken prophetically which only later can be fully understood. This is a good example of a Christocentric understanding of an Old Testament passage. Without Paul's 'theological interpretation', we would not fully understand the words of Isaiah.

Isaiah 54:2-3

"Enlarge the place of your tent,
and let the curtains of your habitations be stretched out;
do not hold back; lengthen your cords
and strengthen your stakes.
For you will spread abroad to the right and to the left,
and your offspring will possess the nations
and will people the desolate cities.

The result of this 'eschatological change', from an 'Israel only' view, to one that accepts Gentiles, would be the transformation of nations.

Isaiah 54:10

For the mountains may depart
and the hills be removed,
but my steadfast love shall not depart from you,
*and my **covenant of peace** shall not be removed,"*
says the LORD, who has compassion on you.

Is the *'covenant of peace'* a reference to the old covenant of Moses? I would say, "No". The context goes back to the first verse in which the Gentiles are to outnumber the people of Israel. This happened with the birth of the church. This covenant of peace is the same covenant that Jeremiah spoke of and which he called *'the new covenant.'*

We know from the book of Galatians that Paul saw new covenant truth in the first verse of Isaiah 54. Is the *"Covenant of Peace"* alluding to a re-worked old covenant, or is it Isaiah's way of proclaiming the new covenant but using different words? Within the context of the chapter, I see no other viable option but to say it is the new covenant. Isaiah is talking about a time of restoration when the people of God come into a covenant which will never be removed. We know from several Scriptures that the old covenant of Moses was never intended to endure forever.

We live in a covenant of peace.

Hebrews 10:1

For since the law has but a shadow of the good things to come instead of the true form of these realities, it can never, by the same sacrifices that are continually offered every year, make perfect those who draw near.

Since the law was a "*shadow*", it was never the full reality of what God desired. The "*good things to come*" are the benefits of the new covenant.

Hebrews 12:18-19

For you have not come to what may be touched, a blazing fire and darkness and gloom and a tempest and the sound of a trumpet and a voice whose words made the hearers beg that no further messages be spoken to them.

The author of Hebrews is very clear. In writing to Christians, he says in essence, "The days of Moses are over, time to move on."

It should be noted that this phrase, "*Covenant of Peace*" is not new to Isaiah. It is used in the book of Numbers and is the term for God's personal covenant to Phinehas, the son of Eleazar and to his family, to have a perpetual priesthood.

Numbers 25:12-13

Therefore say, 'Behold, I give to him my covenant of peace, and it shall be to him and to his descendants after him the covenant of a perpetual priesthood, because he was jealous for his God and made atonement for the people of Israel.'"

Here the "*Covenant of Peace*" cannot be the "new covenant" because it is linked with the old priesthood which became obsolete when the new covenant came. I see this as a special blessing to

Phinehas and not as a covenantal promise that goes outside of his family.

In the book of Ezekiel, the phrase *"Covenant of Peace"* is used once again.

Ezekiel 34:22-25a

I will rescue my flock; they shall no longer be a prey. And I will judge between sheep and sheep. And I will set up over them one shepherd, my servant David, and he shall feed them: he shall feed them and be their shepherd. And I, the LORD, will be their God, and my servant David shall be prince among them. I am the LORD; I have spoken. "I will make with them a covenant of peace. (This word is repeated in Ezekiel 37:24-26)

I would hope there is no doubt that we are dealing with a promise that is fulfilled by the ministry of Jesus. He is the *"David"* that shall feed and care for the sheep. Ezekiel ministered long after King David (over 400 years), yet his hope is in the return of David. God judging between *"sheep and sheep"* may be alluding to the fact that when the true David comes, only the sheep of Israel, those who embrace their Messiah, would be included in this prophecy. The other *"sheep"* - the ones who reject Jesus, would be cut off and come under judgment. All of Israel came into the first century as the sheep of God's pasture; it was their acceptance or rejection of Jesus which would make the difference.

In this passage the term, *"Covenant of Peace"* is again like the one in Isaiah, referring to the peace that would be found in the new covenant.

I like what Alexander McLaren, a Scottish minister (1826-1910), wrote about this verse:

"My covenant of peace.' Dear friends, the prophet spoke a deeper thing than he knew when he uttered these words. Let me remind you of the large meaning which the New Testament puts into them. *'Now the God of Peace that brought again from the dead our Lord Jesus, the Great Shepherd of the Sheep, through the blood of the*

everlasting Covenant, make us perfect in every good work, to do His will.' God has bound Himself by His promise to give you and me the peace that belongs to His own nature, and that covenant is sealed to us in the blood of Jesus Christ upon the Cross."[58]

McLaren writes, "the prophet spoke a deeper thing than he knew." This is the heart of what I call the 'Apostolic Hermeneutic' that must be seen in this and other prophetic passages. We can never know what the Prophet heard from the Holy Spirit and what he understood it to mean; we can only make our evaluation on what he wrote. Yet, whether Ezekiel knew of the fuller significance or not, those of us with the advantage of the New Testament can apply the age-changing ministry of Jesus to this passage.

I like the thought that God gives us the *"peace that belongs to His own nature."*

American theologian Albert Barnes (1798-1870) goes right to the point and declares that Isaiah 54 is a promise for the future Messiah and his people:

"This chapter probably closely connected in sense with the preceding and growing out of the great truths there revealed respecting the work of the Messiah, contains a promise of the enlargement, the moral renovation, and the future glory of the kingdom of God, especially under the Messiah."[59]

Isaiah 54:13

All your children shall be taught by the LORD,
and great shall be the peace of your children.

This passage was covered briefly in chapter three and we remember that when Isaiah predicted, *"For the children of the desolate one will be more than the children of her who is married"*, it meant

---

[58] Alexander McLaren, Expositions of Holy Scripture, Reprinted by Create Space, Forgotten books, 2017
[59] Albert Barnes, Notes on the Bible by Albert Barnes [1834], Text Courtesy of Internet Sacred Texts Archive, Bible Hub

Gentiles will outnumber the children of Israel. It has new covenant applications.

The reason our children will be taught of the Lord is because all members of the body of Christ have the Holy Spirit within them and are living within this *'covenant of peace."*

There is a great deal of Scriptural support that *'peace'* is one of the primary attributes of God. The church needs to be following the character of God as it is a vital aspect of the new covenant.

Isaiah 9:6 Jesus is the *"prince of peace."*

Ephesians 2:13 Apostle Paul says, *"He is our peace,"* and that Jesus *"preached peace."*

Matthew 5:9 *"Blessed are the peacemakers, for they shall be called sons of God.*

Romans 14:17 *"For the kingdom of God is not a matter of eating and drinking but of righteousness and peace and joy in the Holy Spirit.*

II Corinthians 13:11 *"Finally, brothers, rejoice. Aim for restoration, comfort one another, agree with one another, live in peace; and the God of love and peace will be with you."*

The gospel is the message and the lifestyle of peace. Have we forgotten that?

The prophetic word from Isaiah, *"All your children shall be taught by the Lord",* includes the children of Gentiles. This prophecy is being fulfilled in the church, today and in the future generations. This is our hope and vision for the growth of the kingdom of God on the earth.

Several hundred years after Isaiah spoke about the children being taught by the Lord, Jeremiah had a similar line.

Jeremiah 31:34

And no longer shall each one teach his neighbor and each his brother, saying, 'Know the LORD,' for they shall all know me, from the least of them to the greatest, declares the LORD. *For I will forgive their iniquity, and I will remember their sin no more."*

The *"least of them"* certainly includes children. This line follows the prophecy about the 'new covenant.' Not until Jesus came and paid the price, so 'forgiveness of sin' could be offered to all peoples and nations, could this word be fulfilled. It was not fulfilled only in the earthly ministry of Jesus; it is ongoing throughout the kingdom age. This is a prophecy about the people of God being taught by the Lord under the new covenant. How can anyone claim that no Old Testament prophecy is about the church?

The "Covenant of Peace" is the New Covenant.

16. Isaiah 55:1-3

Come, everyone who thirsts,
come to the waters;
and he who has no money,
come, buy and eat!
Come, buy wine and milk
without money and without price.
Why do you spend your money for that which is not bread,
and your labor for that which does not satisfy?
Listen diligently to me, and eat what is good,
and delight yourselves in rich food.
Incline your ear, and come to me;
hear, that your soul may live;
and I will make with you an everlasting covenant,
my steadfast, sure love for David.

Isaiah begins with an unusual offer. He invites people to buy wine and milk for free. He is asking why they are buying bread that does not satisfy. The key to understanding this passage is connecting it to the new covenant where Jesus is our daily bread. The 'everlasting covenant' is the new covenant. We know this because the only covenant that fulfills the Davidic covenant is the new covenant.

The next point to be noticed is that God looks for those who have a need for him. The thirsty and hungry people are welcome at no cost. These are the people that will receive the *sure Mercies of David*. God gave King David a covenant (II Samuel 7:16) and this insured that the house and kingdom of David would last forever. We have in Acts 2 the New Testament commentary on how we should understand this promise. Jesus is the seed of David. He is the one who reigns on David's throne. This is not a physical throne in Jerusalem but is fulfilled by Christ reigning from heaven.

What would the kingdom of Jesus look like without a family? The point of creation is that God would have a people of his own living in the new environment called earth.

We cannot divide the reign of Jesus from the church.

It is the church which continues to release the life and ministry of Christ into the earth. It is the church that is taking the blessings of Abraham to the nations. It is the church that is transforming the nations by proclaiming the kingdom and making disciples. Jesus is king, now and forever. His people are the church, now and forever.

God has established a new covenant, a rich and eternal covenant for those who hunger and thirst after spiritual realities.

17. Isaiah 59:20-21

"And a Redeemer will come to Zion, to those in Jacob who turn from transgression," declares the LORD. "And as for me, this is my covenant with them," says the LORD: "My Spirit that is upon you, and my words that I have put in your mouth, shall not depart out of your mouth, or out of the mouth of your offspring, or out of the mouth of your children's offspring," says the LORD, "from this time forth and forevermore."

Isaiah starts by prophesying the coming of the Messiah. We know this was Jesus. To whom does the Messiah come? He comes to Zion - the people of God, which was Israel. He comes to Jacob which represents the family of Abraham. Even though Jesus came to the nation of Israel we know the majority rejected him (John 1:11). Yet, there would be according to the Prophet, *"Those in Jacob who turn from transgression."* The people of the new covenant will be those from old covenant Israel who turn or repent. This is the remnant that Paul speaks of in Romans 11 (Romans 11:5). The prophet says clearly, *"My covenant with them."* Who are the *"them"*? It is the remnant of Jewish believers who have believed in God's Christ. Later when gentiles are added to the olive tree, we have the church which is neither Jew or Gentile. We have the one new man in the earth; a new creation.

A key element of the coming covenant is the work of the Holy Spirit. It is through the Spirit that the words of God will flow freely from the people of God. How long will this covenant last? *"From this time forth and forever more."* This prophetic word is generational; it goes on and on without end.

Isaiah follows his promise of the Spirit with a statement about his words *"I have put in your mouth."* Is this a separate subject from the giving of His Spirit? This may be a veiled reference to what happened at Pentecost. By looking at this passage through New Testament theology and the coming of the Holy Spirit, I believe this is exactly what we have here. With the coming of the Spirit all believers will speak God's words.

Acts 2:4

And they were all filled with the Holy Spirit and began to speak in other tongues as the Spirit gave them utterance.

Also, keep in mind this is not a one-time event. Isaiah said it was for ongoing future generations. Was this the inspiration for Peter on the day of Pentecost?

Acts 2:39

For the promise is for you and for your children and for all who are far off, everyone whom the Lord our God calls to himself."

If we read this passage in Isaiah without any consideration of the ministry of Christ and the theological understanding of what he accomplished through his death and resurrection, we are left with few viable options. We must either deny what he wrote, claiming it was finished in Christ, or postpone it for our future in the dispensationalist's Millennial kingdom. Both options in my opinion miss the impact of Isaiah's words. They are for us. These powerful words of hope are our inheritance; they are the richness from which the church draws to provide hope and a blueprint for our future.

Repentance would be the key to enable *"Zion"* to receive the message from the *'Redeemer."* This is exactly what Jesus announced.

"Repent, for the kingdom of heaven is at hand (Matthew 4:17).

The church is filled with the Holy Spirit and speaks the words of God.

18. Isaiah 60:1-3

Arise, shine, for your light has come,
and the glory of the LORD *has risen upon you.*
For behold, darkness shall cover the earth,
and thick darkness the peoples;
but the LORD *will arise upon you,*
and his glory will be seen upon you.
And nations shall come to your light,
and kings to the brightness of your rising.

This is a favorite passage of many preachers. Many use these verses to describe the conditions of our current time, which they conclude are the *'last days.'* This is not a prophecy about the darkness of today or a hundred years from now. This is not a prophecy about the second coming of Jesus. What we have is a promise that in a time of darkness the light of God will appear. This is a word of promise for the advent of the Messiah in the first century.

When the Apostles read, *"His glory will be seen upon you"*, they knew it was Jesus in his incarnation and his future ministry. Once their Christ had come, nation after nation would come to the light of the church.

Verse six says camels would come from Midian, Ephah and Sheba. Is this a literal prophecy of treasure coming into ancient Israel? The great evangelist and eighteenth-century reformer, John Wesley, says, "By these, and such like figurative expressions in several verses of this chapter is implied the coming in of all nations to Christ."[60]

How will nations come to the light of the church? The church must be God's image-bearer. We manifest the light that is within us. This is more than a spiritual light, or a moral light; it is also a light of creativity, a light of intelligence, a light of music, a light of science and a light of business. There is no end to how the glory of God will touch the world.

The Church carries the light of God's glory and nations are coming to her brightness.

19. Isaiah 61:1-4

The Spirit of the Lord GOD is upon me,
because the LORD has anointed me
to bring good news to the poor;
he has sent me to bind up the brokenhearted,
to proclaim liberty to the captives,
and the opening of the prison to those who are bound;
to proclaim the year of the LORD's favor,
and the day of vengeance of our God;
to comfort all who mourn;
to grant to those who mourn in Zion—
to give them a beautiful headdress instead of ashes,
the oil of gladness instead of mourning,
the garment of praise instead of a faint spirit;
that they may be called oaks of righteousness,
the planting of the LORD, that he may be glorified.
They shall build up the ancient ruins;

---

[60] John Wesley, John Wesley Explanatory Notes, 1754-65, Amazon Digital Services, LLC, 2013

they shall raise up the former devastations;
they shall repair the ruined cities,
the devastations of many generations.

A summary of this passage could be, 'freedom is coming'. No one can deny this passage has new covenant applications because Jesus quotes Isaiah and says it is fulfilled (Luke 4:18-21). Yet again, dispensationalists go the extra mile to separate a portion of this passage for their version of a future 'Great Tribulation' and their '1,000-year Millennium.' Since Jesus stopped reading after announcing the *"Year of the Lord's favor"* they presume the rest of the passage is separate and will be fulfilled in our future. This is poor exegesis and results in a bad hermeneutic. The *"day of vengeance"* came in the first century when the Temple and the city of Jerusalem was destroyed in the fall of 70 AD. Jesus spoke often of this throughout the gospels. The Apostles spoke often of a coming judgment. Just because Jesus did not read the entire prophecy of Isaiah does not mean he was giving it separate interpretations.

Those living in the new covenant are called *"oaks of righteousness."* This righteousness is strong. It endures the storms. It stands for generations.

The church has a charge from God to repair culture. We are to be engaged with the broken-hearted. We have the answers for the rebuilding of our cities. The church has the answers for those who are weak and are in mourning. We are to lift people up and give them the *"oil of gladness"* and *"the garment of praise."*

When the Church teaches 'Righteousness' we will begin to repair the devastations of many generations.

20. Isaiah 61:11

For as the earth brings forth its sprouts,
and as a garden causes what is sown in it to sprout up,
so the Lord GOD will cause righteousness and praise
to sprout up before all the nations.

If we misread the first few verses of Isaiah 61, we will also misinterpret this verse. When will the Lord bring about *"righteousness and praise"* in the nations? It did not happen under the old covenant. Again, only as we apply a theological understanding can we accurately see the full truth of these types of passages.

How will *"righteousness and praise"* sprout up in the nations? We need to see this is not the type of righteousness which was found under the Mosaic Law. Apostle Paul is writing about those under the law, that they *"were ignorant of the righteousness of God."*

Romans 10:1-4

Brothers, my heart's desire and prayer to God for them is that they may be saved. For I bear them witness that they have a zeal for God, but not according to knowledge. For, being ignorant of the righteousness of God, and seeking to establish their own, they did not submit to God's righteousness. For Christ is the end of the law for righteousness to everyone who believes.

Paul makes a fascinating statement about how the Jews were *"ignorant"* of God's righteousness. How could that be? They knew the Law of God; they followed every word of Moses. Yet, they totally missed what righteousness was about. Who was the *"righteousness of God"* they missed? It was Jesus. Christ was the goal (the end) of the Law.

Any attempt to interpret Isaiah 61 without the theology of Christ's righteousness, is missing the key prophetic element.

The book of Hebrews says, that without holiness, no one shall see the Lord (Hebrews 12:14). How much does it take? Is 10% holy enough? How about 30%? What if we achieve 99%? The problem is, we have attempted to be holy by our works. We have thought (wrongly) that by separating ourselves from the world we could be more holy. We thought by going to church we would become holy. We created rule after rule to follow, thinking that if we kept enough of them, we would be holy. None of this creates holiness. Righteousness and holiness are found in Jesus. It is his holiness that we need. If you want to be 100% holy, then receive the holiness of Jesus. Make an exchange – give your failures, your religious works and your sins to Jesus, so that he can put them all to death, and embrace what is offered – his forgiveness and his righteousness. Through Jesus we see God!

These are our roots. Do not give them away!

The kingdom grows by the righteousness of Christ, manifested through the church.

21. Isaiah 65:17-25

For behold, I create new heavens
and a new earth,
and the former things shall not be remembered
or come into mind.
But be glad and rejoice forever
in that which I create;
for behold, I create Jerusalem to be a joy,
and her people to be a gladness.
I will rejoice in Jerusalem
and be glad in my people;
no more shall be heard in it the sound of weeping
and the cry of distress.
No more shall there be in it
an infant who lives but a few days,
or an old man who does not fill out his days,
for the young man shall die a hundred years old,
and the sinner a hundred years old shall be accursed.
They shall build houses and inhabit them;
they shall plant vineyards and eat their fruit.
They shall not build and another inhabit;
they shall not plant and another eat;
for like the days of a tree shall the days of my people be,
and my chosen shall long enjoy the work of their hands.
They shall not labor in vain

or bear children for calamity,
for they shall be the offspring of the blessed of the LORD,
and their descendants with them.
Before they call I will answer;
while they are yet speaking I will hear.
The wolf and the lamb shall graze together;
the lion shall eat straw like the ox,
and dust shall be the serpent's food.
They shall not hurt or destroy
in all my holy mountain,"
says the LORD.

Our exegetical task in this amazing and intriguing passage is to determine as best we can, the meaning of *"For behold, I create new heavens and a new earth."* Everything will flow out from how we interpret the meaning and timing of this *'new heaven and earth.'* Isaiah provides not only prophetic words, but a vision for these future days. Scholars and non-scholars alike have been puzzled by this passage and there have been several interpretations.

A Reformed Amillennial view by David J. Engelsma:

"Isaiah 65:17ff. is not about the present world, Jerusalem, Jews, long and trouble-free earthly lives, nice houses, good farms, plenty of money, ease, happy times, and tame wolves. It is about Jesus Christ, His church, salvation, eternal life, and a new, different world. It is about a *spiritual* Christ, a *spiritual* people, *spiritual* salvation, *spiritual* blessings, *spiritual* life, and a *spiritual* world."[61]

Second, we have an interpretation from a Dispensational view. John A. Martin wrote in *The Bible Knowledge Commentary*:

"In these verses the Lord described the millennial kingdom, which is seemingly identified here with the eternal state (new heavens and a new earth). In Revelation, however, the new heavens and new

---

[61] David J. Engelsma, Reformed Amillennialism – A Spiritual Interpretation of Isaiah 65:17ff., http://graceonlinelibrary.org/eschatology/amillennialsm/ reformed-amillennialism-a-spiritual-interpretation-of-isaiah-6517ff-by-prof-david-j-engelsma/

earth (Revelation 21:1) follow the Millennium (Revelation 20:4). Most likely Isaiah did not distinguish between these two aspects of God's rule; he saw them together as one. After all, the Millennium, though 1,000 years in duration, will be a mere pinpoint of time compared with the eternal state."[62]

Poor Isaiah! From the dispensational view, he comes across as confused because he is unable to distinguish between the 'Millennium' kingdom and the eternal state. I would suggest that Isaiah was not confused because he failed to see a 1,000-year millennial kingdom but he was giving birth to a vision - a 'God breathed' vision, of the kingdom age which would begin when the Messiah would come. Isaiah did not make any distinctions, because for him there was one kingdom, which was to come; not two. Isaiah was not a 'Premillennialist.'

Bible Teacher John MacArthur:

"New heavens and a new earth. Israel's future kingdom will include a temporal kingdom of a thousand years (see notes on Revelation 20:1–10) and an eternal kingdom in God's new creation (51:6,16; 54:10; 66:22; cf. Revelation 21:1–8).[63]

I will quote one more Dispensationalist - a well-known one - Cyrus Scofield (you now know his first name):

"Verse 17 looks beyond the kingdom-age to the new heavens and the new earth... but verses 18–25 describe the kingdom-age itself. Longevity is restored, but death, the "last enemy" (1 Corinthians 15:26), is not destroyed till after Satan's rebellion at the end of the thousand years (Revelation 20:7–14)."[64]

---

[62] John A. Martin, *The Bible knowledge commentary: An exposition of the scriptures*, (1:1120). Wheaton, IL: Victor Books.

[63] MacArthur, J. J. (1997, c1997). The MacArthur Study Bible (electronic ed.) (Is 65:17). Nashville: Word Pub.

[64] Scofield, C. I. (2002). The Scofield study Bible (Is 65:17). New York: Oxford University Press.

The Dispensational position is that Isaiah is prophesying a two-stage development of God's future. He sees a 1,000-year Millennial kingdom, followed by the 'eternal state.' Also, we need to notice that the 1,000-year kingdom is for Israel; it is not for the church.

A Third Alternative

Is there another way to understand the words of Isaiah? Yes, there is. Allow me to quote myself from my book *Glorious Kingdom*:

"Isaiah reveals a picture of a peaceful, glorious time upon earth, everyone being productive and fruitful. This is not describing heaven, but the blessings of heaven on earth. This is not describing a time 'post-resurrection' either, because death still occurs. The events described here are part of our age and show the direction the world is heading."[65] Even if there is an element of symbolism, what does it symbolize? Isaiah speaks of a time of great peace, a time of joy and long life. This is the kind world we are heading toward. The work is not finished. We have work to do. Just as we are saved and there remains a work in our hearts and minds, the beginning stages of the 'new heaven and new earth' is not the end. The kingdom continues to advance and in time no one will question if we are living in God's new earth; it will be clear for all to see.

The "New Heavens and New Earth" began with the New Covenant.

22. Jeremiah 23: 5-6

Behold, the days are coming, declares the LORD, when I will raise up for David a righteous Branch, and he shall reign as king and deal wisely, and shall execute justice and righteousness in the land. In his days Judah will be saved, and Israel will dwell securely. And this is the name by which he will be called: 'The LORD is our righteousness.'

---

[65] Stan Newton, Glorious Kingdom, Vision Publishing, Ramona, Ca., 2012, page 67

We saw plenty of references to "David" from Isaiah. Here, several hundred years later, Jeremiah still speaks about God raising up a new David. The Prophets were not teaching the reincarnation of David, but a David-like King who would rule the nations. This new King would establish true righteousness and justice. What is the Kingdom of God? It begins with righteousness (Romans 14:17). Those in Christ are made righteous. Once we stop attempting to be righteousness, stop striving to be holy (mostly by religious legalistic standards) and accept that we are as righteous as we will ever be, the kingdom on earth will advance. It is not our actions that create righteousness, but the work of Christ in us, giving us his righteousness. Yes, we can proclaim with great joy - *"The Lord is our righteousness."*

The Righteous Branch is Jesus and He is our Wise King.

23. Jeremiah 30:3, 7-9

For behold, days are coming, declares the LORD, when I will restore the fortunes of my people, Israel and Judah, says the LORD, and I will bring them back to the land that I gave to their fathers, and they shall take possession of it."

Alas! That day is so great there is none like it; it is a time of distress for Jacob; yet he shall be saved out of it. "And it shall come to pass in that day, declares the LORD of hosts, that I will break his yoke from off your neck, and I will burst your bonds, and foreigners shall no more make a servant of him. But they shall serve the LORD their God and David their king, whom I will raise up for them.

If we are convinced that a literal hermeneutic is the only method to interpret Scripture, we will be expecting a restoration of Israel to the land promised to Abraham.

Father of modern dispensationalism, John Darby (1800-1882), connects these verses to Matthew 24 and Mark 13:

"The day of Jacob's trouble: promised deliverance and sure judgment. Some details of the circumstances that accompany its exercise deserve our attention, as well as the character which God displays in it, and the extent of its effects. In chapter 30 God commands Jeremiah to write in a book all the words of the judgment which he had heard, for God would restore the people. Now this deliverance found Israel at the height of the distress. This is the first thing presented to the prophet. No day could be compared to this day of Jacob's trouble. It is the day spoken of in Matthew 24 and Mark 13."[66]

Those familiar with Darby's theology know that he sees these events in the future - in the *"last days."* I am not a fan of Darby's eschatology but at least he gets it right, that these events relate to Jesus' prophecy in Matthew 24 (also in Mark 13 and Luke 21). The difference is, I view the words and signs given by Jesus in these passages as all pointing to the destruction of the temple and the city of Jerusalem, which took place in the first century. The *"day of Jacob's trouble"* is history. We see *"David"* again, which is a familiar Old Testament way to describe the Messiah. The believers living in Jerusalem during this time heeded the words of Jesus and escaped the city right before its destruction.

This is a prophetic word which had its beginning with the people of God being restored by accepting their Messiah and then goes past the time that the New Testament was written. Once we get past 70 A.D., we have wonderful prophecies about the general conditions of the advancing kingdom, but we also have words that relate only to a particular event and time.

In the ministry of Jesus and the church, the New Testament Apostles saw the regathering of the people of Israel.

24. Jeremiah 30:22-24

And you shall be my people,
and I will be your God."
Behold the storm of the LORD!
Wrath has gone forth,

---

[66] John Darby, Synopsis of the Books of the Bible, Believers Bookshelf Canada, Inc., 2005

a whirling tempest;
it will burst upon the head of the wicked.
The fierce anger of the LORD will not turn back
until he has executed and accomplished
the intentions of his mind.
In the latter days you will understand this.

The greatest of all promises for God's people is the establishment of our relationship with him. We are the people of God and God acts in accordance with this truth. Yet, as in many passages, there is a counter balance to the blessings that are coming - there is also judgment. We must keep this tension alive as we interpret the Prophets. The first century was a time of blessings and fulfillment, as well as one of great judgment. It was the birth of the new covenant and the ending of the old covenant. It was both a time of new life flowing from God's new creation people and the time of the '*Great Tribulation.*'

We cannot separate the day of blessings from the day of the Lord, which brought forth judgment upon unbelieving Israel. Those who rejected Jesus as the Christ, were cut off from the Olive Tree.

The "Last Days" were days of Judgment and Blessings.

25. Jeremiah 31:33-34

*For this is the covenant that I will make with the house of Israel after those days, declares the LORD: I will put my law within them, and I will write it on their hearts. And I will be their God, and they shall be my people. And no longer shall each one teach his neighbor and each his brother, saying, 'Know the LORD,' **for they shall all know me, from the least of them to the greatest,** declares the LORD. For I will forgive their iniquity, and I will remember their sin no more.*"

There are critical questions that must be asked concerning this remarkable prophecy from Jeremiah. "Which people receive this promised new covenant?" "What 'Law' does Jeremiah refer to?" Again, without applying an Apostolic Hermeneutic (by using the basic principles of a Christocentric and Theological Hermeneutic), we will end up with a Zionist position. We already covered '*The Israel of God*' and therefore should conclude that this new covenant is for believing Jews and Gentiles. It is the people of Christ's Church that receive the new covenant.

The other question that is often forgotten when addressing this passage is, "What Law will be placed in the hearts of God's people?" If we conclude it is the Mosaic Law, then the nature of the church would be radically different than what we see taught by Jesus and the Apostles. Here, a Theological Interpretation of Scripture is necessary. The new covenant replaces the old covenant. And with a change of covenants, there is also a change of law.

Hebrews 7:12

For when there is a change in the priesthood, there is necessarily a change in the law as well.

I Corinthians 9:19-20

For though I am free from all, I have made myself a servant to all, that I might win more of them. To the Jews I became as a Jew, in order to win Jews. To those under the law I became as one under the law (though not being myself under the law) that I might win those under the law. To those outside the law I became as one outside the law (not being outside the law of God but under the law of Christ) that I might win those outside the law.

Apostle Paul clears up any confusion about what 'Law' those belonging to Christ are under. Paul is not under the old Mosaic Law, but under the "Law of Christ." The "Law of Christ" is the Law of God for new covenant members.

Apostolic Interpretation of Jeremiah's New Covenant:

1. The people receiving the new covenant are those of the new creation - the church. We are the 'Israel and Judah', that fulfill the promise.
2. The "Law" which is written in our hearts, is the "Law of Christ."

The New Covenant is the great Equalizer, "They shall All Know Me."

26. Jeremiah 33:14-18

Behold, the days are coming, declares the LORD, when I will fulfill the promise I made to the house of Israel and the house of Judah. In those days and at that time I will cause a righteous Branch to spring up for David, and he shall execute justice and righteousness in the land. In those days Judah will be saved, and Jerusalem will dwell securely. And this is the name by which it will be called: 'The LORD is our righteousness.' "For thus says the LORD: David shall never lack a man to sit on the throne of the house of Israel, and the Levitical priests shall never lack a man in my presence to offer burnt offerings, to burn grain offerings, and to make sacrifices forever."

After the second temple was destroyed by the Romans in the first century, there have not been any "*burnt offerings.*" It is verses like this that provide a bit of comfort to the advocates of a 'Premillennial Kingdom'. Should we expect, based on passages like this, that '*burnt offerings*' shall be part of our future? The New Testament has the final say - Jesus was the final sacrifice. Returning to any type of sacrifice would be denying the gift of God's Son to be the offering for the entire world.

Hebrews 7:26-27

For it was indeed fitting that we should have such a high priest, holy, innocent, unstained, separated from sinners, and exalted above the heavens. He has no need, like those high priests, to offer sacrifices daily, first for his own sins and then for those of the people, since he did this once for all when he offered up himself.

The promise from Ezekiel that there shall be '*burnt offerings*' forever must come under the fresh revelation of the Apostles, based upon the work of Jesus at the cross. It is finished. Sin has been dealt with. If you have embraced Jesus as God's Messiah and believe he brought him alive from the dead, then, you are now righteous. You will never be 'more righteous.' We do not need a future offering of any kind; Jesus made the final one and it was fully accepted by the Father.

The Throne of David is now Occupied and Always will be.

27. Jeremiah 49:34-39

The word of the LORD that came to Jeremiah the prophet concerning Elam, in the beginning of the reign of Zedekiah king of Judah. Thus says the LORD of hosts: "Behold, I will break the bow of Elam, the mainstay of their might. And I will bring upon Elam the four winds from the four quarters of heaven. And I will scatter them to all those winds, and there shall be no nation to which those driven out of Elam shall not come. I will terrify Elam before their enemies and before those who seek their life. I will bring disaster upon them, my fierce anger, declares the LORD. I will send the sword after them, until I have consumed them, and I will set my throne in Elam and destroy their king and officials, declares the LORD. "But in the latter days I will restore the fortunes of Elam, declares the LORD."

We have here what we see in many Old Testament passages. The Prophet is declaring God's judgment upon people and nations, followed by words of restoration. This time the people of Elam are in view. The Prophets declare disaster upon the people *"until I have consumed them."* Then, at the end of the prophetic declaration there is hope; *"In the latter days I will restore the fortunes of Elam."*

How will Elam be restored? What will this look like? When we go to the book of Acts, we find out.

Acts 2:4-12

And they were all filled with the Holy Spirit and began to speak in other   tongues as the Spirit gave them utterance. Now there were dwelling in Jerusalem Jews, devout men from every nation under heaven. And at this sound the multitude came together, and they were bewildered, because each one was hearing them speak in his own language. And they were amazed and astonished, saying, "Are not all these who are speaking Galileans? And how is it that we hear, each of us in his own native language? Parthians and Medes *and **Elamites** and residents of Mesopotamia, Judea and Cappadocia, Pontus and Asia, Phrygia and Pamphylia, Egypt and the parts of Libya belonging to Cyrene, and visitors from Rome, both Jews and proselytes, Cretans and Arabians—we hear them telling in our own tongues the mighty works of God." And all were amazed and perplexed, saying to one another, "What does this mean?"*

The promise of the Spirit is repeated several times in the Old Testament. At the Day of Pentecost, the followers of Jesus received what Jesus told them to wait for - the promised Holy Spirit. This was the start of their being the new Israel. This, as they would come to understand, meant they were the sons of Abraham; they now had a David-like king in Jesus. All the promises for old covenant Israel were now available within the new covenant. It was different. Things have changed. Yet, the promises were elevated to greater heights.

Who was among those hearing the good news from Apostle Peter? Elamites were there. God fulfilled the promise made by the Prophet. Restoration, not again as a political nation, but the true restoration - restoration to God through Jesus. Restoration now came by way of the Holy Spirit and living in the new covenant.

To take this passage and attempt to force a political restoration is beyond its purpose. I do not believe the Prophets spoke about modern nations. Even though there are those attempting to see Russia, China, United States, Iran, Syria, and yes, even modern-day Israel as fulfilling prophecy in some fashion, I do not see this as a valid method of interpreting the Bible. The nations we see listed in Scripture were those having dealings with old covenant Israel. It was the known world then. The far-a-way nations of ancient China or Central American countries were not in the view of the Prophets, as they had no known association with Israel. Also, the core of the Bible's Message - the arrival of God's Christ and his kingdom came to pass. This is the end of the Bible's written story. We have the promises and prophecies that continue in the church, but we are now writing our story. The work of Christ is finished. Ours is only beginning. All nations throughout history and even into the future can benefit by the promises given.

Those experiencing the new covenant will expand into every nation. All nations will see God's glory. All nations will come and worship the King. This is the message and hope of the kingdom. Yet, this is different than saying a specific nation is the focus of Biblical prophecy.

God kept his promises to the Elamites and those promises that remain to be fulfilled in their fullness, will also be fulfilled.

28. Ezekiel 21:25-27

And you, O profane wicked one, prince of Israel, whose day has come, the time of your final punishment, thus says the Lord GOD: Remove the turban and take off the crown. Things shall not remain as they are. Exalt that which is low, and bring low that which is exalted. A ruin, ruin, ruin I will make it. This also shall not be, until he comes, the one to whom judgment belongs, and I will give it to him.

Ezekiel speaks to the final king of Judah - Zedekiah, and declares his days are ending, so there's a demand that he removes his crown. God is finished with the long reign of human kings. They were not his choice, but the peoples', going back to the days of Samuel. Things are going to change. Verse 27 is the key. We need to identify the "*He*" who is to come. There will be another king, there will be a person, who will receive the crown. Historically, there was no other king to replace Zedekiah. The next king was Jesus the Christ.

Joseph Benson, an early Methodist in England and close associate to John Wesley, states clearly who the '*He*' is, "*I will overturn, overturn, overturn it* — By several degrees I will utterly overthrow the kingdom of Judah; *and it shall be no more* — It shall never recover its former luster and dignity; *until he come,* — Till the Messiah come to take his kingdom."[67]

In the gospel of Luke, the promise of a kingly throne is restated:

Luke 1:32-33

He will be great and will be called the Son of the Most High. And the Lord God will give to him the throne of his father David, and he will reign over the house of Jacob forever, and of his kingdom there will be no end."

Bible Scholar Matthew Poole (English Nonconformist Theologian (1624-79):

"It shall be no more; never recover its former glory and strength, but consume, till the scepter be quite taken away from Judah, and way be made for the Messiah, who is he that is to come, whose is the dominion, and to whom the Father will give it. So, the final desolation of the temporal kingdom of the seed of David, which was most heavy tidings to the carnal Jews, is threatened, and the eternal kingdom of the Messiah, most joyful tidings to the believing Jews, is promised."[68]

God has spoken through his prophet. The judgment against human kings has now come. Yet, there will be another king and He will wear the crown of God's authority. There will be another king that will rule in righteousness. Finally, John the Baptist cries out the day is near; the Kingdom of God is at hand. Will Israel receive their new king? Those first-century Jews who recognized Jesus as their Christ gladly became part of God's re-organized Israel (around his Messiah and not the Torah) and those who refused him were part of the final

---

[67] Joseph Benson, The Holy Bible Containing the Old and New Testaments with Critical, Explanatory and Practical Notes, Volume I, II and III (Old Testament, Complete), 1849, George Lane & Levi Scott, publishers, 1849

[68] Matthew Poole, Matthew Poole's Commentary on the Holy Bible, Hendrickson Publishers, Peabody, Massachusetts, U.S.A. (1985)

judgment against unbelieving Israel. They were no longer part of the "Israel of God (Galatians 6:16)."

The Church has a King and His Kingdom is in Session.

29. Ezekiel 36:24-28

I will take you from the nations and gather you from all the countries and bring you into your own land. I will sprinkle clean water on you, and you shall be clean from all your uncleannesses, and from all your idols I will cleanse you. And I will give you a new heart, and a new spirit I will put within you. And I will remove the heart of stone from your flesh and give you a heart of flesh. And I will put my Spirit within you, and cause you to walk in my statutes and be careful to obey my rule. You shall dwell in the land that I gave to your fathers, and you shall be my people, and I will be your God.

Ezekiel writes a passage where the exegete needs to dig a little deeper. It is passages like this where a 'Christocentric or Theological Interpretation' is necessary to fully grasp the prophecy and how it is being fulfilled.

The dispensational literal approach is easy to determine. They would claim this prophecy is about what will happen in the '*last days*' of the church age, when God will reassemble Israel back to the land, cleanse them from sin, give them a new heart and put his Spirit in them. They will then dwell in the land God promised Abraham; living in peace. Why not interpret it in this fashion? Ezekiel's words are straight forward.

There are several key reasons why a 'literal' hermeneutic does not work here. We will examine them one at a time and then see how the whole of the prophecy must be viewed from a new covenant perspective. We will attempt to mine out the truth from Ezekiel's prophecy.

Let's begin with verse 24, where God promises to bring them back to the land. Is the return of Israel in 1948 the fulfillment of this prophecy? I do not believe it is for several reasons.

As we read these five verses (24-28), we notice there are similarities to the prophecy by Jeremiah concerning the new covenant (Jeremiah 31:31). Now, if we agree that the new covenant prophecy of Jeremiah is for natural Israel and not for the church, then we remain consistent. But, if we see the prophecy of Jeremiah as being fulfilled in Christ and applied to the church, it follows that Ezekiel's words would match.

In the new covenant there is cleansing from sin and receiving of the Spirit. Apostle Paul may have had Ezekiel's words in mind, when he wrote to the Corinthians.

II Corinthians 3:3

And you show that you are a letter from Christ delivered by us, written not with ink but with the Spirit of the living God, not on tablets of stone but on tablets of human hearts.

This did not happen to natural Israel as a nation but to those Jews and Gentiles, that embraced Jesus as God's Messiah. This is new covenant truth that is expressed throughout the New Testament.

When did this first occur? When did the Spirit of God fall upon the people of God in the new covenant era? Who was present? Where were they?

Acts 2:4

When the day of Pentecost arrived, they were all together in one place. And suddenly there came from heaven a sound like a mighty rushing wind, and it filled the entire house where they were sitting. And divided tongues as of fire appeared to them and rest on each one of them. And they were all filled with the Holy Spirit and began to speak in other tongues as the Spirit gave them utterance.

The followers of Jesus received the *"Promise of the Father"* and now were fully ushered into the grace of the new covenant. Who else was transformed and received a 'new heart' and the 'Spirit' of God? Jews from around the nations were gathered for the keeping of Pentecost.

Acts 2:5-13

Now there were dwelling in Jerusalem Jews, devout men from every nation under heaven. And at this sound the multitude came together, and they were bewildered, because each one was hearing them speak in his own language. And they were amazed and astonished, saying, "Are not all these who are speaking Galileans? And how is it that we hear, each of us in his own native language? Parthians and Medes and Elamites and residents of Mesopotamia, Judea and Cappadocia, Pontus and Asia, Phrygia and Pamphylia, Egypt and the parts of Libya belonging to Cyrene, and visitors from Rome, both Jews and proselytes, Cretans and Arabians—we hear them telling in our own tongues the mighty works of God." And all were amazed and perplexed, saying to one another, "What does this mean?" But others mocking said, "They are filled with new wine."

What did Ezekiel say? He said God will gather them from the nations and put his Spirit in them. Ezekiel's prophecy was fulfilled on the Day of Pentecost when the Holy Spirit fell, baptizing them all into the body of Christ - the church.

Another interesting aspect is to see how Apostle Paul understands the promise to Abraham, concerning the land. Under the old covenant it was limited to a small piece of geography but under the new covenant, it expanded to cover the whole earth.

Romans 4:13

For the promise to Abraham and his offspring that he would be heir of the world did not come through the law but through the righteousness of faith.

This is a clear example of how the New Testament Apostles applied a 'Theological Interpretation" to the land promises in the Old Testament. For the authors of the New Testament the old covenant become void at the cross when the curtain to the Holy of Holies was opened. As the age progressed even the actual practice of Temple worship, with all its old covenant requirements would soon disappear and become obsolete. (Hebrews 9:13).

The words of Ezekiel came true and are still being fulfilled as people across the nations embrace the Messiah and receive the gift of the Holy Spirit. The land we possess is what we stand on. The whole earth is His.

Possess your Holy Land!

30. Ezekiel 37:21-22, 24-28
The Dry Bones Prophecy

The prophecy about the dry bones has been a favorite topic for sermons. It has all the elements that help create a dramatic sermon. Therefore, since it is well-known, I will not address the complete story of the bones coming alive and becoming a great army but concentrate on the eschatological meaning - the coming of a new David to be their united king.

Then say to them, Thus says the Lord GOD: Behold, I will take the people of Israel from the nations among which they have gone, and will gather them from all around, and bring them to their own land. And I will make them one nation in the land, on the mountains of Israel. And one king shall be king over them all, and they shall be no longer two nations, and no longer divided into two kingdoms.

"My servant David shall be king over them, and they shall all have one shepherd. They shall walk in my rules and be careful to obey my statutes. They shall dwell in the land that I gave to my servant Jacob, where your fathers lived. They and their children and their children's children shall dwell there forever, and David my servant shall be their prince forever. I will make a covenant of peace with them. It shall be an everlasting covenant with them. And I will set them in their land and multiply them, and will set my sanctuary in their midst forevermore. My dwelling place shall be with them, and I will be their God, and they shall be my people. Then the nations will know that I am the LORD who sanctifies Israel, when my sanctuary is in their midst forevermore."

In passages like this, it seems clear that God will unite the twelve tribes and bring them back to their chosen land. Are we still waiting, after 2700 years, for the ten tribes of Israel to return and be joined with Judah? No, we are not! This was fulfilled on the day of Pentecost. Unless we see these types of 'restoration prophecies' through the apostolic hermeneutic, we will create all sorts of bizarre interpretations about the 'lost tribes.' It is time to stop searching for the 'lost tribes.' They are not lost. The family of God is united in Christ. We are the Israel of God (Gal. 6:16).

The Old Testament is written and centered around old covenant Israel. Its language, its poems and even the prophetic words take on this 'Israel centered' speech. Once we get to the New Testament we must, if we are to agree with the Apostles of Jesus, come to a 'new covenant' understanding of these passages. If we are to benefit and enjoy our 'Rich Root', being informed by this interpretation is necessary.

Alexander MacLaren (1826-1910), an English non-conformist from Scotland:

"We may extend the application of the vision to the condition of humanity and the divine intervention which communicates life to a dead world, but must remember that no such meaning was in Ezekiel's thoughts... The great work of the gospel is to communicate divine life. The details of the process in the vision are not applicable in this respect. As we have pointed out, they are shaped after the pattern of the creation of Adam, but the essential point is that what the world needs is the impartation from God of His Spirit. We know more than Ezekiel did as to the way by which that Spirit is given to men."[69]

MacLaren makes two comments worth noting. He begins with an important hermeneutical principle that we need to understand. Even if it seems right to interpret Ezekiel's vision as pertaining to our Christian experience, which I believe it is, this does not mean it is what Ezekiel had in mind. This is a key principle of a 'Theological Interpretation.' We are not limited to the 'historical circumstances'

---

[69] Alexander MacLaren, MacLaren's Expositions of Holy Scripture, Baker Pub Group, 1988

of when the Prophets spoke. We have the advantage of seeing these words, inspired by the Spirit from the position of the finished work of Christ. Therefore, we can see more than what Ezekiel saw. And this is MacLaren's second point; we have more knowledge and experience from the Holy Spirit than Ezekiel. Our position in Christ helps us understand how we should interpret this passage and other similar ones in the Old Testament.

The key is when Ezekiel declares David will be their prince forever. King David of old had been dead for hundreds of years, yet the hope of Israel was fixed on a David-like King to return. Jesus is their Prince. He will reign forever. Should we as followers of Jesus be waiting for a future event (His Second Coming), to receive him as king? Here is where the New Testament is clear. Once the resurrection took place, it was the sign for the new believers to know that God had made Jesus both our savior and king and that he was the one spoken of whenever 'David" was mentioned in the Old Testament.

Acts 1:29-36

"Brothers, I may say to you with confidence about the patriarch David that he both died and was buried, and his tomb is with us to this day. Being therefore a prophet and knowing that God had sworn with an oath to him that he would set one of his descendants on his throne, he foresaw and spoke about the resurrection of the Christ, that he was not abandoned to Hades, nor did his flesh see corruption. This Jesus God raised up, and of that we all are witnesses. Being therefore exalted at the right hand of God, and having received from the Father the promise of the Holy Spirit, he has poured out this that you yourselves are seeing and hearing. For David did not ascend into the heavens, but he himself says, " 'The Lord said to my Lord, "Sit at my right hand, until I make your enemies your footstool." ' Let all the house of Israel therefore know for certain that God has made him both Lord and Christ, this Jesus whom you crucified."

Once the resurrection took place and the followers of Jesus were filled with the Holy Spirit, they knew Jesus was the Messiah and King.

We must read the Old Testament, especially passages like this in Ezekiel through the lens of Christ and the new covenant.

The Dry Bones of Every Nation shall come alive and join the New Covenant People of God.

31. Ezekiel 38:1-3

Ezekiel begins this section with a prophecy about God and Magog.

The word of the LORD came to me: "Son of man, set your face toward Gog, of the land of Magog, the chief prince of Meshech and Tubal, and prophesy against him and say, Thus says the Lord GOD: Behold, I am against you, O Gog, chief prince of Meshech and Tubal.

Many evangelicals have negative feelings toward Russia based upon Ezekiel's statement that God is *"against"* this land called *"Magog."* This has been the standard dispensational interpretation. C.I. Scofield, "That the primary reference is to the northern (European) powers, headed up by Russia, all agree."[70] Well, Mr. Scofield, not all agree, in your day nor ours.

Many older commentaries see this as God's final judgment that stands against God's true Israel, the church.[71] Others interpret it as being fulfilled during various historical conflicts, including the time of the Maccabees.[72] Our purpose here is not to exegete this passage or others dealing with judgment of nations at the end of time or in

---

[70] C.I. Scofield, Scofield Reference Notes to the Bible, 1907 Notes, CreateSpace Independent Publishing Platform

[71] Albert Barnes, Barnes Notes on the Old and New Testament, Baker Books, 1983

[72] A. R. Fausset, David Brown, Robert Jamieson, Jamieson, Fausset, and Brown's Commentary on the Whole Bible, GLH Publishing ,June 9, 2012

our past but to see how these judgment passages should be seen by using a Christocentric hermeneutic.

Are there nations predestined for God's wrath? Are there nations, which are '*goat*' or '*sheep*' nations? It is necessary that we read these Old Testament passages in view of the new covenant. Did the cross of Jesus alter God's declarations of judgment on these nations?

Jesus spoke about Goat and Sheep nations, or did he?

Matthew 25:31-34

When the Son of Man comes in his glory, and all the angels with him, then he will sit on his glorious throne. Before him will be gathered all the nations, and he will separate people one from another as a shepherd separates the sheep from the goats. And he will place the sheep on his right, but the goats on the left. Then the King will say to those on his right, 'Come, you who are blessed by my Father, inherit the kingdom prepared for you from the foundation of the world.

In a passage like this it becomes too easy to inject modern theological concepts, which would have been foreign to the audience Jesus was speaking to. We should not immediately jump to an end-time rapture or engage in end of the world discussions. Does Jesus use this language of coming in glory, coming with angels and sitting on a throne in other places? Yes, he does, and it would behoove us to grasp the meaning of these passages before interpreting the above one.

Matthew 10:23

When they persecute you in one town, flee to the next, for truly, I say to you, you will not have gone through all the towns of Israel before the Son of Man comes.

Here we have Jesus telling his disciples he will come. How will he come? He will come in "*clouds*" with "*angles*" and in "*his kingdom.*" When will he come? Before the disciples - the same followers he was speaking to - finished their work of preaching in the villages of Judea. However, we try to interpret this *"coming of the Son of man"* we know it occurred within one generation.

Matthew 16:27-28

For the Son of Man is going to come with his angels in the glory of his Father, and then he will repay each person according to what he has done. Truly, I say to you, there are some standing here who will not taste death until they see the Son of Man coming in his kingdom."

When we go back to our text in Matthew 25, we can use the previous sayings of Jesus to help understand the passage. First, we should notice that Jesus never said he would judge nations for being sheep or goats. He says he will separate "people" from all the nations. There is no such concept that nations are to be separated according to a *"goat"* or *"sheep"* nation. Second, a closer look is needed to see if this is an end of time judgment or it happened when Jesus said his coming as the Son of man would occur, which is a coming within one generation.

Does Ezekiel predict a final judgment, where *"Magog"* will be judged? I do not see that as part of God's final design under the new covenant.

Under the New Covenant there are no *"Goat"* nations, *"All the families of the nations shall worship before you"* (Psalm 22:27).

32. Ezekiel 39:28-29

Then they shall know that I am the LORD their God, because I sent them into exile among the nations and then assembled them into their own land. I will leave none of them remaining among the nations anymore. And I will not hide my face anymore from them, when I pour out my Spirit upon the house of Israel, declares the Lord GOD."

God's promise to pour out his Spirit is a common theme throughout the Old Testament. It is a key factor which separates the new from the old covenant. All the promises made by Ezekiel are fulfilled by

Jesus and in his advancing kingdom. This includes the regathering of Israel, that God would turn his face towards them and pour out his Spirit upon them.

The fulfilment of the God's promise "When I will pour out my Spirit" was on the day of Pentecost. Then, after several years, the same 'Spirit' was poured out on Gentiles.

Israel and Judah were regathered to the land and received the Holy Spirit on the Day of Pentecost.

33. Ezekiel 47 The River

Ezekiel 47:1, 3-6, 12

Then he brought me back to the door of the temple, and behold, water was issuing from below the threshold of the temple.

Going on eastward with a measuring line in his hand, the man measured a thousand cubits, and then led me through the water, and it was ankle-deep. Again he measured a thousand, and led me through the water, and it was knee-deep. Again he measured a thousand, and led me through the water, and it was waist-deep. Again he measured a thousand, and it was a river that I could not pass through, for the water had risen. It was deep enough to swim in, a river that could not be passed through. And he said to me, "Son of man, have you seen this?"

And on the banks, on both sides of the river, there will grow all kinds of trees for food. Their leaves will not wither, nor their fruit fail, but they will bear fresh fruit every month, because the water for them flows from the sanctuary. Their fruit will be for food, and their leaves for healing."

Ezekiel was a Prophet of visions. His visions are a good test for our method of interpretation. I remember listening to a pastor that held to a literal river coming out of a rebuilt temple. When we force a literal interpretation, we end up believing bizarre circumstances and events. I do not believe in a real river coming out of a physical building. We miss Ezekiel's point, which is the increase of the Holy

Spirit's activity in the earth over time. The temple is the church. The Holy Spirit flows out from his people not out of physical structures. We should also take notice that the river does not come from governmental buildings, or presidential palaces, or educational libraries, or business institutions. God will restore our human intuitions as we first allow the life-changing, miracle-working power of the Holy Spirt to flow freely within us. God's river of his Spirit flows from his house. The transformation of nations starts within each of us and through the church. We need a continual flow of the river and we need a flow that increases. The greatest need in the church today is this ever-increasing, life-giving river of the Holy Spirit.

Psalms 46:4

There is a river whose streams make glad the city of God, the holy habitation of the Most High.

In and around the temple mount there were a few streams and springs, but never a river, especially a mighty river, as Ezekiel sees. Of course, the dispensational literal approach sees this as a future event. They believe God will create a river which flows out from the new temple.

Zechariah 14:8

On that day living waters shall flow out from Jerusalem.

Both Zechariah and Ezekiel prophesied about a river, that shall flow out of Jerusalem or the temple. Yes, there is a river that provides joy for the people of God and that river is what Jesus spoke of in the gospel of John.

John 7:37

On the last day of the feast, the great day, Jesus stood up and cried out, "If anyone thirsts, let him come to me and drink. Whoever believes in me, as the Scripture has said, 'Out of his heart will flow rivers of living water.'" Now this he said about the Spirit, whom those who believed in him were to receive, for as yet the Spirit had not been given, because Jesus was not yet glorified.

Jesus refers to Scripture for his promise of living water. What Scripture?

Biblical scholar Craig Keener:

"Jewish tradition suggests that on the last day of the Feast of Tabernacles, priests read to the people from Zechariah 14 and Ezekiel 47, which talk of rivers of living water flowing forth from the Temple in the end time. Jesus is now speaking on the last day of that feast (7:2, 37), probably alluding to the very Scriptures from which they had read ("as the Scripture said," 7:38). Jewish people thought of the Temple as the "navel" or "belly" of the earth. Therefore, Jesus may be declaring, "I am the foundation stone of the new temple of God. From me flows the water of the river of life; let the one who wills come and drink freely!"[73]

According to Keener, it was tradition on the final day of the feast to read from two prophets - Zechariah 14 and Ezekiel 47. How does Jesus interpret these prophecies? He does not read them literally, as in a real river, but speaks of the Holy Spirit. It is the Spirit that gives life to wherever it touches. Jesus takes the words of the Old Testament Prophets and applies, if I may say, a 'Christocentric' understanding. We should do no less.

The River of God is flowing from His Church to the Nations.

34. Daniel 2:1, 12-13, 31-45

In the second year of reign the reign of Nebuchadnezzar, Nebuchadnezzar had dreams; his spirit was troubled, and his sleep left him.

The King of Babylon had a dream. You can find it in chapter 2, it is about a large statute with four distinguishable parts. In the following verses, Daniel gives the King the interpretation:

"This was the dream. Now we will tell the king its interpretation. You, O king, the king of kings, to whom the God of heaven has given

---

[73] Craig Keener, http://www.craigkeener.com/rivers-of-living-water-in-john-737-38

the kingdom, the power, and the might, and the glory, and into whose hand he has given, wherever they dwell, the children of man, the beasts of the field, and the birds of the heavens, making you rule over them all—you are the head of gold. Another kingdom inferior to you shall arise after you, and yet a third kingdom of bronze, which shall rule over all the earth. And there shall be a fourth. And in the days of those kings the God of heaven will set up a kingdom that shall never be destroyed, nor shall the kingdom be left to another people. It shall break in pieces all these kingdoms and bring them to an end, and it shall stand forever, just as you saw that a stone was cut from a mountain by no human hand, and that it broke in pieces the iron, the bronze, the clay, the silver, and the gold. A great God has made known to the king what shall be after this. The dream is certain, and its interpretation sure."

The four parts of the statue represent four great empires. In the traditional understanding, it begins with Babylon and ends with the Roman Empire in the first century, with the Medes/Persians and the Greek empire in between. This fourth kingdom, the days of the Roman Empire are when God acts and establishes his own kingdom. The days of humans having final control will come to an end; God will take over and his kingdom shall have no end. How does God establish his rule over the earth? Through his Son - Jesus the Christ. This is the good news. This is our story to the nations. Jesus has come, defeated sin, death and Satan, rose from the dead and has received all authority in heaven and on earth. Therefore, in my opinion, there will never be a world dominating empire again. The final kingdom - the fifth kingdom - is the kingdom of God, and it has no rival. There is no competition and Jesus rules over the nations, marching toward total victory.

The key to understanding Daniel's interpretation of the king's dream is the timing of the fifth kingdom. If we postpone it, by necessity we must have a 'revived Roman empire.' We must recreate first-century conditions, so God can establish his kingdom on earth. Common sense, at least it seems to me, is to accept the New Testament assertions that with the coming of Jesus, the kingdom of God - the one Daniel saw - arrived on the earth and has been increasing ever since.

The Fifth and final world empire began with the Incarnation of Jesus.

35. Daniel 7:9-10

As I looked, thrones were placed,
and the Ancient of Days took his seat;
his clothing was white as snow,
and the hair of his head like pure wool;
his throne was fiery flames;
its wheels were burning fire.
A stream of fire issued
and came out from before him;
a thousand thousands served him,
and ten thousand times ten thousand stood before him;
the court sat in judgment,
and the books were opened.

Daniel saw the Ascension of Jesus. Was it by a vision, or did he travel in the future to witness the events firsthand? We do know that he saw one of the most important events in human history; the day Jesus was officially crowned king of the universe. These opening verses set the stage for what comes later. The Ancient of Days is the Father. As He takes his seat the court is in session. I would love to see that on film. Maybe with virtual reality we can someday begin to catch the grandeur, splendor and the beauty of this awesome event. Maybe if we could see it visually the doctrine of the Ascension and the present kingdom of God on earth would be more appreciated by the church. Once the stage is set, the Son of Man makes his appearance.

"I saw in the night visions,
and behold, with the clouds of heaven
there came one like a son of man,
and he came to the Ancient of Days

and was presented before him.
And to him was given dominion
and glory and a kingdom,
that all peoples, nations, and languages
should serve him;
his dominion is an everlasting dominion,
which shall not pass away,
and his kingdom one
that shall not be destroyed.

I have been preaching the Ascension based upon Daniel's description for several decades. I see this grand celebration as the time Jesus is officially given kingship by his Father. This is the coronation of Jesus. He is given the kingdom and the glory to rule over the nations.

The Ascension of Jesus was His Coronation as King of all Creation.

36. Hosea 3:4

For the children of Israel shall dwell many days without king or prince, without sacrifice or pillar, without ephod or household gods. Afterward the children of Israel shall return and seek the LORD *their God, and David their king, and they shall come in fear to the* LORD *and to his goodness in the latter days.*

Once again, we are faced with the dilemma about how these prophetic words should be interpreted. A literal approach doesn't fit with the revelation of the new covenant Apostles. How will God's people return to King David, when he has been dead for a thousand years? David must be interpreted as Christ. He is Israel's true king. David was a type of the Messiah. We have many references in the Bible to the *"fear of the Lord"* and have come to a healthy knowledge that it does not mean we live afraid of our God, but that we have awesome respect for the One and True God. Yet, Hosea adds a phrase, God's people will *"seek"* their God and come to His *"Goodness."* The *"Goodness"* of God is expanded and truly revealed in the new covenant. When does all this take place? It happens in the "*latter days*." The "*last days*" of the old covenant, the time Jesus came to earth and the time of the early church - these are the "*last days*." Hebrews makes this clear.

Hebrews 1:1-2

Long ago, at many times and in many ways, God spoke to our fathers by the prophets, but in these last days he has spoken to us by his Son, whom he appointed the heir of all things, through whom also he created the world.

The Goodness of God has now come to all people.

37. Joel 2:28-29

And it shall come to pass afterward,
that I will pour out my Spirit on all flesh;
your sons and your daughters shall prophesy,
your old men shall dream dreams,
and your young men shall see visions.
Even on the male and female servants
in those days I will pour out my Spirit.

There is no dispute about when this prophecy was fulfilled. On the day of Pentecost, Apostle Peter stood before the people and declared Joel's prophecy was happening. The timing of fulfillment was in the 'last days.' *Pulpit Commentary* makes this point:

"And it shall come to pass afterward…This intimates the **time** when the promised blessing is to be bestowed, and must be read in the light of New Testament exposition; for Peter, in quoting the words (Acts 2:17, etc.), varies the prophet's note of time by substituting an explanatory phrase… "in the last days" - an expression which, as is acknowledged, refers to the days of the Messiah or the last days of the old dispensation."[74]

---

[74] Pulpit Commentary, H. D. M. Spence, Joseph S. Exell, Wm. B. Eerdmans Publishing Company; 1978 PRINTING edition

The Holy Spirit was poured out in the '*last days*.' The term '*last days*', as used in the Bible, is connected to the final generation of the old covenant and the time Israel's Messiah comes to earth.

The extraordinary freedom exhibited by the New Testament Apostles can be seen in how Peter removes words from Joel and replaces them with words from Isaiah. What he does is remove the words "*after this*" from Joel and replace them with "*last days*" from Isaiah. Peter wanted no misunderstanding about what was taking place - this was what Joel prophesied. This is an excellent example of an Apostolic Hermeneutic.

G.K. Beale remarks on this exchange of words:

"The first time the wording "last days" appears in the NT (in canonical order) is Acts 2:17, where Peter explains, "And it shall be in the last days,' God says, 'that I will pour forth My Spirit upon all mankind; and your sons and your daughters shall prophesy.'" Here Peter understands that the tongues being spoken at Pentecost are the beginning of Joel's end-time prophesy that a day would come when God's Spirit would gift not merely prophets, priests, and kings, but all classes of people in the covenant community would "prophesy" (Acts 2:15-17a; cf. Joel 2:28-29). At the beginning of the Joel quotation, Peter substitutes the phrase "in the latter days" in place of Joel's "after these things." The substitution comes from Isaiah 2:2-3."[75]

Special Note: The New Testament Apostles were moved by the Holy Spirit and were writing what would become part of the inspired cannon. No one today should be removing words of Scripture and replacing them with different ones. Yet, what we do learn is how they applied their new 'theology' to what the Old Testament Prophets said.

---

[75] G.K. Beale, A New Testament Biblical Theology, Baker Academic, Grand Rapids, Michigan, 2011, p. 136

Joel 2:30-31

And I will show wonders in the heavens and on the earth, blood and fire and columns of smoke. The sun shall be turned to darkness, and the moon to blood, before the great and awesome day of the LORD comes.

Should we divide Joel's prophesy into two parts? Should we see the outpouring of the Holy Spirt as being fulfilled on the Day of Pentecost and then interpret verse 30-31 as taking place in the distance future from the first century? No, we need to see how they were all fulfilled in the period Peter calls the *"last days."* All agree that the first section about the pouring out of the Holy Spirit occurred on the day of Pentecost in the first century. Yet, once again, the doctrines of dispensationalism place a large gap of time between verse 29 and verse 30. This is done to keep the *"Great Tribulation"* in our future and not in the first century. The events of verse 30 took place 40 years later, when the Romans destroyed the Jewish temple and the city of Jerusalem. It was still in the time of the *'last days.'* The only difference is that Pentecost took place towards the beginning of the *"last days"* and the judgment took place towards the conclusion of the *'last days."*

The prophetic language of the Old Testament is used to describe a nation losing its light and influence. It was indeed a day of darkness, because around 1,000,000 people were killed. Yet, those embracing Jesus as the Messiah, escaped to the mountains and were saved. They survived what Jesus called the *'Great Tribulation'* (Matthew 24:21).

John Gill makes the connection between verse 30 and the events that followed 40 years after the day of Pentecost:

"And I will show wonders in the heavens and in the earth, this, and what follow, refer to the prodigies seen in the air, and done in the earth, a little before the destruction of Jerusalem; when in the air were seen comets and blazing stars, particularly one in the form of a sword, hanging over Jerusalem, and appearances of armies engaged in battle; and, on the earth, a flame was seen in the temple."[76]

Some claim that everything of the Old Testament is fulfilled in the person and ministry of Jesus. I do not like the word 'fulfilled' because it has the sense of everything being over. My understanding is that all the Old Testament speaks of Jesus and points to him as the one delivering us out of bondage and darkness, transferring us into the kingdom and the new covenant. Through his death and resurrection, he takes all the promises and sets them on a higher plane of fulfillment. If Joel's prophecy were only fulfilled in the person of Jesus, why was the Spirit not poured out at his baptism, instead of upon the church at Pentecost? Pentecost could not happen until Jesus opened the realm of heaven through the cross. So, it was fulfilled and keeps on being fulfilled in and through the church. The church is fulfilling the prophecy of Joel. The kingdom of God is powered by the Holy Spirit. The Kingdom of God is life in the Holy Spirit.

The New Testament Apostles are the final and authoritative interpreters of the Old Testament.

38. Amos 9:11-15

"In that day I will raise up
the booth of David that is fallen
and repair its breaches,
and raise up its ruins
and rebuild it as in the days of old,
that they may possess the remnant of Edom
and all the nations who are called by my name,"
declares the LORD who does this.
"Behold, the days are coming," declares the LORD,
"when the plowman shall overtake the reaper

---

[76] John Gill, Gill's Commentary and Exposition of the Old and New Testaments, Baker Book House, 1980

and the treader of grapes him who sows the seed;
the mountains shall drip sweet wine,
and all the hills shall flow with it.
I will restore the fortunes of my people Israel,
and they shall rebuild the ruined cities and inhabit them;
they shall plant vineyards and drink their wine,
and they shall make gardens and eat their fruit.
I will plant them on their land,
and they shall never again be uprooted
out of the land that I have given them,"
says the LORD your God.

Amos gives us a perfect example. Reading this 'literally' would conclude the following:

A. Old Testament Israel will return to the land promised by Abraham and resume animal sacrifices.

B. When Israel returns to the land, their crops will be supernaturally blessed.

C. The physical temple will be raised up and resemble Solomon's Temple.

This is exactly how dispensationalists interpret the words of Amos. The problem is we have the new covenant apostolic commentary in the book of Acts. When Apostle James brings to conclusion the discussion whether Gentiles are to keep the Jewish laws to be saved, he totally ignores any literal interpretation of Amos and applies the restoration of Israel to the church.

The Apostles used a Christocentric interpretation and a theological interpretation, to understand Amos. This is our task. We do not have the Apostles to guide us in every passage, but we are not without help; we have the Holy Spirit. As the Holy Spirit helped the Apostles, he will help us.

At the council of the Apostles and elders in Acts 15, James quoted the Prophet Amos as a support to Gentiles being added to God's new covenant people. Since Gentiles were now embracing Israel's

Messiah and were being grafted into the olive tree, should they therefore continue to keep the Mosaic Law? It seemed logical. Gentiles '*in Christ*' had become one with Israel and everyone knew Jews kept the laws of Moses. So, when these 'Gentiles' became part of the newly organized Israel (around their Messiah - Jesus), were they to be recognized as 'Jews' keeping the law of Moses?

The dispute in Acts 15 never addressed the larger question, "As Jews, who have entered the new covenant, are we free from the Mosaic Law?" Their only question was about these believing Gentiles. Should they keep the law? It was not until later and mainly through Apostle Paul that the question of the validity of the Law was addressed where Jews were concerned. The revelation of the new covenant grew, but not without resistance. It was not until the Temple was destroyed and the whole of Jewish religious life taken away, that Christians, Gentiles and Jews alike, knew they were free from the Mosaic Law.

The Kingdom of God is a day of a continuous miracle harvest.

39. Micah 3:12

Therefore because of you
Zion shall be plowed as a field;
Jerusalem shall become a heap of ruins,
and the mountain of the house a wooded height.

Micah was a contemporary of Isaiah. His ministry was from 742 to 686 B.C. He prophesied before the Northern Kingdom fell (721 B.C.). His audience was the people of Samaria and those in Jerusalem. Micah lived during the time of three kings of Judah - Jotham (750-732), Ahaz (735-713) and Hezekiah (716-687). Hosea, Amos and Isaiah were prophesying during the time of Micah.

"Zion will be plowed as a field." These words remind us of the events, which occurred after the destruction of Jerusalem in 70 A.D. We know from history this is exactly what happened. Yet, is this what Micah was speaking about, or was it the destruction of the city by Babylon?

"The city fell in 586 BC: "[Nebuchadnezzar] burned the house of the LORD and the king's house and all the houses of Jerusalem; every great house he burned down."[77]

A wide field of commentaries take a common view of this prophecy. Benson is an example: "There is nothing which hinders us from referring this prophecy to the first destruction of Jerusalem (586 BC) …The prophecy, however, may have a further respect to the total destruction of Jerusalem when Terentius Rufus, by the order of Titus, ploughed up the very foundations of it."[78]

We need to interpret Micah's words as pertaining to the judgment that was pending. Yet, when we apply the Apostolic understanding, the judgment on Jerusalem and the temple must not be ignored since it had the most significant theological overtones (the destruction in 70 A.D.).

Clarke takes a similar view but goes directly to the events in the first century as more likely the primary fulfillment. He applies what we are calling a Christocentric or a Theological Interpretation:

"Thus did the Romans treat Jerusalem when it was taken by Titus. Turnus Rufus, or as he is called by St. Jerome, Titus Arinius Rufus, or Terentius Rufus, according to Josephus, caused a plough to be drawn over all the courts of the temple to signify that it should never be rebuilt, and the place only serve for agricultural purposes. See the note on Matthew 24:2. Thus Jerusalem became heaps, an indiscriminate mass of ruins and rubbish; and the mountain of the house, Mount Moriah, on which the temple stood, became so much neglected after the total destruction of the temple, that it soon resembled the high places of the forest. What is said here may apply also, as before hinted, to the ruin of the temple by Nebuchadnezzar in the last year of the reign of Zedekiah, the last king of the Jews."[79]

---

[77] S. Michael Houdmann, CEO, Got Questions, https://www.gotquestions.org/about.html

[78] Joseph Benson, Benson's Commentary, G. Lane & C.B. Tippett, 1846

[79] Adam Clarke, Clarke's Commentary, Abingdom Press, 1831

The Prophet is blaming someone, when he says, *"Because of you"*. Who is responsible for the coming destruction? It was mostly the leaders, including priests and prophets. The common people were to blame too. For any immediate destruction that occurred within their generation, those contemporaries of Micah carried the blame, yet, in the larger picture they were one of many generations which contributed to the final destruction of the temple. When we read the words of Jesus, they bring home the memory of what Micah foresaw hundreds of years earlier.

Woe to you, scribes and Pharisees, hypocrites! For you build the tombs of the prophets and decorate the monuments of the righteous, saying, 'If we had lived in the days of our fathers, we would not have taken part with them in shedding the blood of the prophets.' Thus you witness against yourselves that you are sons of those who murdered the prophets. Fill up, then, the measure of your fathers. You serpents, you brood of vipers, how are you to escape being sentenced to hell? Therefore I send you prophets and wise men and scribes, some of whom you will kill and crucify, and some you will flog in your synagogues and persecute from town to town, so that on you may come all the righteous blood shed on earth, from the blood of righteous Abel to the blood of Zechariah the son of Barachiah, whom you murdered between the sanctuary and the altar. Truly, I say to you, all these things will come upon this generation (Matthew 23:29-36).

"Fill up, then, the measure of your fathers." The final generation of covenant Israel had the ultimate decision to make. Was Jesus Yahweh's Christ? Their leaders along with the masses of the nation answered, "No" and the weight of sin from all previous generations came upon them. They were the reason Jerusalem would be plowed like a field.

Those who claim all Old Testament prophecies are fulfilled in Christ and have therefore no continuing fulfillment after him, should at least admit that this prophecy was fulfilled some forty years after the earthly ministry of Jesus was completed. Jesus prophesized this event and it was recorded in three gospels; Matthew 24, Mark 13 and Luke 21. The prophecy came through him but found its fulfillment years later.

The final Judgment upon National Israel is in the past. There is no ongoing curse or threat of destruction; today is the day of salvation.

40. Micah 4:1-4

It shall come to pass in the latter days
that the mountain of the house of the LORD
shall be established as the highest of the mountains,
and it shall be lifted up above the hills;
and peoples shall flow to it,
and many nations shall come, and say:
"Come, let us go up to the mountain of the LORD,
to the house of the God of Jacob,
that he may teach us his ways
and that we may walk in his paths."
For out of Zion shall go forth the law,
and the word of the LORD from Jerusalem.
He shall judge between many peoples,
and shall decide disputes for strong nations far away;
and they shall beat their swords into plowshares,
and their spears into pruning hooks;
nation shall not lift up sword against nation,
neither shall they learn war anymore;
but they shall sit every man under his vine and under his fig tree,
and no one shall make them afraid,
for the mouth of the LORD of hosts has spoken.

The context takes us back into chapter 3. The theme is judgment. The prophet makes a case against Judah and Israel, charging them with crimes such as the leaders taking bribes and prophesying for money. Then, in verse 12 he proclaims, *"Therefore because of you Zion shall be plowed as a field; Jerusalem shall become a heap of ruins, and the mountain of the house a wooded height."* From a Christocentric perspective the events of Jerusalem being destroyed, and the temple being burned in 70 A.D., is the New Testament understanding of what Micah was describing.

Again, we have an example, where what the author (Micah) most likely meant, has a deeper and more meaningful fulfillment. He prophesies events which made the visible old covenant vanish forever. In any good exegesis it is always proper to begin with, "What did the author mean and what did the readers understand it to mean?" Nevertheless, in these prophetic passages we see the fulfillment is often beyond the scope of the prophet, so the interpretation from the Apostolic point of view works best.

This prophecy is almost identical to one given by Isaiah (Isaiah 2:1-5). The question arises, "Who gave the original?" Or, did they individually, prompted by the Spirit, give the same prophecy? Although this is possible, the leaning among scholars is "the preponderance of opinion is in favor of Micah being regarded as the original writer."[80]

This passage describes conditions in the age of the Messiah - the kingdom age, which began in the first century. Zion, the spiritual center of God's purposes is one of preeminence. This is the church; God's people on the earth. We are the new temple which connects heaven and earth. The nations (mountains) of the world come willingly to experience the presence and peace of God. When we speak of transforming nations, we must be mindful that they will be eager to come and be transformed. This is not a takeover or forced conversion. When God is moving through his people to such a degree, where his love, peace and justice are attractive to the world, then the nations will come to Zion.

We can also observe that as this age of the kingdom advances, there remain independent nations. We are not headed towards a one-world government. Over time nations will freely submit to King Jesus. God has a plan for the nations and he will use the church to execute

---

[80] Charles J. Ellicott, Ellicott's Bible Commentary For English Readers, Delmarva Publications

his will on the earth. Who will be the ones that create workable peace plans for nations in conflict? It will be the church. God will raise up people, who will come to a place of authority and governmental leaders will listen. God will give insight to prophets, who will give answers to serious conflicts. This has already begun to a minor degree.

The prophet Micah saw nations coming to Zion and being taught the word of God. That is the path we are on.

Micah is a prophet, who gives us an amazing blueprint for the advancing kingdom.

The Glorious Church is being established as the Highest Mountain.

41. Habakkuk 2:1-4

And the LORD answered me:
"Write the vision;
make it plain on tablets,
so he may run who reads it.
For still the vision awaits its appointed time;
it hastens to the end—it will not lie.
If it seems slow, wait for it;
it will surely come; it will not delay.
"Behold, his soul is puffed up; it is not upright within him,
but the righteous shall live by his faith.

Habakkuk was told to write down the vision. Why? So those whose job it was to spread the message, would have a clear and authoritative word.

The prophet declared that the vision *"awaits its appointed time."* John Grill comments on the latter part of that phrase, *"It hastens to the end."*

"Should be rendered not "it" but "he" and so the apostle has taught us to interpret it of a person, and not a thing, that is, "at the end" of the time appointed, or at the end of the Jewish state, both civil and ecclesiastic, the Messiah should appear, as he did, which is called the end of the world."[81]

From the words of Habakkuk, Grill sees a promise that the Messiah will come at the end of the Jewish state. I agree. When will that happen? The book of Hebrews gives us the answer:

Hebrews 9:26 (KJV)

For then must he often have suffered since the foundation of the world: but now once in the end of the world hath he appeared to put away sin by the sacrifice of himself (KJV).

The King James Version has the word, "world" twice in this verse. The Greek word for the physical earth is 'Kosmos" and is the correct translation for the first usage. Yet, looking at the 'Mounce Reverse-Interlinear New Testament', we find the second usage is incorrect.

Mounce translates the English word world as first the "Kosmos" and then the second time as "aion."

As we can see, the word "aion" means 'an age', not the end of the world. Jesus came at the end of the 'aion' - the end of the Jewish age.

The Vision for the Church is recorded; "Go therefore and make disciples of all nations (Matthew 28:19).

42. Habakkuk 2:14

For the earth will be filled
with the knowledge of the glory of the LORD
as the waters cover the sea

Habakkuk declares God's ultimate purpose for the earth. When Jesus came to earth, he knew his place was to bring "Glory" to God and yet it was the Father who gave his Son "Glory" (Daniel 7:14). In John 17, Jesus prays, *"Father, the hour has come; glorify your Son that the Son may glorify you* (John 17:1). Jesus knew his time

---

[81] John Gill, Gills Commentary an Exposition of the Old and New Testament, Baker Book House, 1980

on earth was almost completed. Why does Jesus pray that he be 'glorified'? He wants the ability to give 'glory' back to the Father. How did Jesus glorify his Father while on earth? "*I glorified you on earth, having accomplished the work that you gave me to do* (John 17:4)." Glory is connected to the work of ministry. We miss the full impact of 'God's Glory' when we link it only to worship. To advance the kingdom to the place God desires it will take work. Thoughtful, faithful, and Spirit-filled work.

Towards the end of Jesus' prayer, he says to his Father, "*The glory that you have given me I have given to them, that they may be one even as we are one* (John 17:22)". The Father gives Jesus his glory. The Son glorifies the Father. The followers of Jesus receive that, which was given to the Son. All this leads to oneness. To advance the kingdom of God in the earth and see His glory cover the earth like the Prophet spoke, we must find unity in our work of ministry. This has proven to be difficult. Yet, it must always be our goal. We need to find ways to engage in ministry, in unity with other believers and leaders.

Seeing God's glory cover the earth is not some magical dream of those disconnected from the work of ministry. As great as worship is, as vital as worship is, the church must be involved in the work of ministry. This work of ministry should engage in every sphere of life. This is the purpose of leadership in the church - equipping the saints for the work of the ministry (Ephesians 4:12).

This verse in Habakkuk has fueled my heart with fire throughout my life. It has released an unending love for the Scriptures. It has been the foundation for my 'kingdom revelation.' We can only imagine what a world filled with the glory of God will look like, yet, one thing I am sure of - it will be far greater and more glorious than we can imagine.

The Earth is Filled NOW with God's Glory; the mission of the Church is to increase the knowledge of this truth.

43. Zephaniah 3:9

*For at that time I will change the speech of the peoples
to a pure speech,
that all of them may call upon the name of the LORD
and serve him with one accord.*

Zephaniah was a contemporary of King Josiah – 640 B.C. – 609 B.C. The word given to Zephaniah was one of warning, followed by the hope of restoration. He lived after the fall of the northern kingdom (Israel) and before the fall of Jerusalem (Judah) to Babylon. Alongside Zephaniah were Prophets Jeremiah and Habakkuk.

A major theme of Zephaniah is the "Day of the Lord." It is mentioned 17 times. A day of wrath, fire and judgment needed to be spoken and Zephaniah was the one chosen to proclaim it. Yet, the book is not all doom and gloom for the people of God, it ends with a common theme among the prophets - restoration.

How should the astute student of the Bible understand the restoration portions of Zephaniah? Is this only about those, who returned to Jerusalem after the Babylonian captivity? Or, as in other prophetic passages, the prophet is seeing something beyond his time and declaring a larger restoration that is to come?

I have heard it taught, that this is a prophecy about the recovery of the Hebrew language. It coincides with Israel becoming a nation in 1948 and therefore is a sign of the soon coming of Jesus. This is standard dispensational thinking. Are there other options? What is this *"pure speech"* Zephaniah writes about?

It says that this *"pure speech"* will facilitate a unity in worship. God's people will come together and serve him *"with one accord."* I see this happening on the day of Pentecost. I see speaking in pure form, not in human speech, but a speech, which is under the influence of the Holy Spirit.

Acts 2:1-4

When the day of Pentecost arrived, they were all together in one place. And suddenly there came from heaven a sound like a mighty rushing wind, and it filled the entire house where they were sitting. And divided tongues as of fire appeared to them and rested on each one of them. And they were all filled with the Holy Spirit and began to speak in other tongues as the Spirit gave them utterance.

The passage is not clear enough to be dogmatic, yet, I see the great day of Pentecost as fulfilling this prophecy. It was then that God's new people - the church - were filled with the Holy Spirit and began taking the gospel to the nations.

The Advance of the Kingdom needs a people filled with Holy Spirt and walking in unity.

44. Zephaniah 3:17

The LORD your God is in your midst,
a mighty one who will save;
he will rejoice over you with gladness;
he will quiet you by his love;
he will exult over you with loud singing.

Joseph Parker (1830-1902), an English Congregational minister says about verse 17; "This is more than the usual Hebrew reduplication of words; it means that the divine heart and the human heart are one; it means that the Gospel has prevailed over sin, and that earth is being lifted up day by day to the very gate of heaven."[82]

We see here the words of love and victory. The kingdom age has come, and King Jesus is with his people, singing loudly over his church. This reminds me of Hebrews 1:9, where the author says of Jesus, *"therefore God, your God, has anointed you with the oil of gladness beyond your companions."*

---

[82] Joseph Parker, The People's Bible, Forgotten Books, 2018

These words can be said of any people, of any time. It was true in the old covenant and what needs to be considered is how the new covenant makes every promise better. We do live in the better covenant. Better, because even the old promises are taken to a higher realm, where we experience them like they should be, in a relationship with God, through Christ and lived out by the Holy Spirit.

Jesus is in the midst of His church, singing and rejoicing over us.

45. Haggai 2:6-9

The Prophet's name means "festival, feast, or festive", therefore, it has been suggested he may have been born on one of the Jewish feast days. All we know of Haggai is that he most likely was born in Babylon during the time of the captivity. The Scripture tells us nothing about his father or family. He may have been a child and returned to Jerusalem with his family, along with the 50,000 who came with Zerubbabel (536 B.C.). By adding together all the known factors, we can say his prophecy was close to the year 520 B.C.

In an interesting note, when the group of 50,000 with Zerubbabel returned to Jerusalem, there was a small population living there. These were the few that Babylon left behind to live in the ruins of the city. They began to marry foreigners around them. This group, made up of Jews and other nationalities, became known as the Samaritans.

The message of Haggai was to proclaim *"Go up to the hills and bring wood and build the house, that I may take pleasure in it and that I may be glorified, says the LORD* (Haggai 1:8). The people responded and *"and they came and worked on the house of the LORD of hosts, their God (*Haggai 1:14) Yet, when the building was completed the older generation saw it was inferior to Solomon's Temple. *"Who is left among you who saw this house in its former glory? How do you see it now? Is it not as nothing in your eyes?* (Haggai 2:3)

Despite its failure to match what Solomon had built, the Prophet foretold of a greater glory coming.

Haggai 2:6-9

For thus says the LORD of hosts: Yet once more, in a little while, I will shake the heavens and the earth and the sea and the dry land. And I will shake all nations, so that the treasures of all nations shall come in, and I will fill this house with glory, says the LORD of hosts. The silver is mine, and the gold is mine, declares the LORD of hosts. The latter glory of this house shall be greater than the former, says the LORD of hosts. And in this place I will give peace, declares the LORD of hosts.'"

Now, we are faced with the task of interpreting this passage in a Christocentric way. Are we to understand that *"this house"* - the Second Temple (Herod greatly expanded it in his day) - will in the future receive a greater glory? We have the luxury of reading about the fate of the '*latter temple*" in the first century and it was anything but a house of greater glory. Jesus had words for the temple in his days and they were not good. How are we to understand these words of the Prophet?

The Prophet sees a day, where *"the treasures of all nations shall come in."* A study Bible makes an interesting comment:

"Though the Hebrew term translated "treasures" could refer to a person (i.e., the Messiah), the immediate context here favors a reference to the things desired by all nations (i.e., the things precious to them). Verse 8 speaks of such precious things, and the decree of King Darius, during whose reign Haggai ministered, alludes to precious things being contributed to the temple building project (Ezra 6:3–5, 8–9). Here Haggai probably echoes Isaiah's promise of an Israel made rich by the wealth of the nations (Isaiah 60:5). In other words, he speaks of the Messianic age."[83]

The word "treasures" can be a reference to the Messiah. One cannot be certain, but Messianic undertones are indeed here. Therefore,

---

[83] Reformation Study Bible, Ligonier Ministries, 2015, Haggai 2

since we are dealing with a prophecy of the "Messiah's Kingdom", we know the temple to be filled with *"greater glory"* is not a physical building, but the new creation temple - the church. This 'Theological Interpretation' is strengthened by the author of the book to the Hebrews.

Hebrews 12:26-28

At that time his voice shook the earth, but now he has promised, "Yet once more I will shake not only the earth but also the heavens." This phrase, "Yet once more," indicates the removal of things that are shaken—that is, things that have been made—in order that the things that cannot be shaken may remain. Therefore let us be grateful for receiving a kingdom that cannot be shaken, and thus let us offer to God acceptable worship, with reverence and awe, for our God is a consuming fire.

The Prophet Haggai is quoted and is offered as a proof text for the coming of the Kingdom of God, which cannot *"be shaken."* Because we are grateful for this kingdom, we are to worship God in an acceptable fashion. The book of Hebrews builds a case, chapter after chapter, for the superiority of Christ over the old priesthood and the fact that the new covenant is replacing the soon to be extinct old covenant. The worship we offer is not worship in the 'latter temple' of Herod, but the glorious new temple of the church.

The words of Haggai, *"Yet once more, in a little while, I will shake the heavens and the earth",* should be viewed as the old covenant being removed. This is the time that the kingdom arrived with the Messiah (Mark 1:14-15).

What do we learn from Haggai? The glory of the King's Temple - Jesus and his church - is declared to be more glorious than any previous temple.

The Church is God's Temple of the Kingdom age.

46. Zechariah 1:17

The book of Zechariah is important to our greater understanding of the kingdom. The New Testament authors quote the Prophet 71 times. If we are to understand the present kingdom of God, the writings of Zechariah cannot be ignored. While we are eager to engage with the Prophet's words, we also need to recognize the interpretation of many passages are highly disputed and not always easy to understand. For those who want to dig deeper, you will be rewarded. It deserves a full-length book. For our purposes here, we can only highlight a few passages.

Before looking at specific passages, a brief historical introduction would be helpful. The King of Babylon, Nebuchadnezzar, conquered Jerusalem in the year 587 B.C. and demolished the temple.

Bakers Evangelical Dictionary of Theology

William B. Nelson, Jr.

"Many scholars also connect the second section of Zechariah with Malachi because Zechariah 9-11, Zechariah 12-14, and Malachi all begin with the word "oracle." Alternately, some scholars argue that chapters 9-14 were composed by Zechariah, but at a later time in his life, exiling many of Judah's leaders to Babylon. After a time God raised up Cyrus, the Persian king, to defeat Babylon (539) and to release the Jews from captivity by issuing an edict in 538 allowing them to return to their land. Not only did he liberate them; he returned the temple vessels that Nebuchadnezzar had plundered and gave them permission to rebuild their temple with Persian funds (Ezra 6:3-5). Theological Themes. Building for Christ. Christians emphasize the spiritual world and the second coming of Christ to such an extent that they neglect material needs. The Book of Zechariah shows the importance of this world. It affirms the necessity of human institutions, political structures, and mundane things such as buildings. In order for the Jews to reestablish themselves in the land, they had to rebuild the temple and restore the priesthood; they also had to set up a form of governance. We are also members of Christian societies: local churches, denominations and parachurch organizations. We can encourage the building of houses of worship, hospitals, rescue missions, mental health centers, food distribution centers and shelters for the homeless, the battered and unwed mothers. In addition, we should construct Christian schools, colleges, and theological seminaries for the purpose of training Christian leaders."[84]

Nelson provides an important application from our reading of Zechariah. I like his comment, "The Book of Zechariah shows the importance of this world." Since God's kingdom is already on the earth and is prophesied to grow, our mindset should be not, "How fast can we get to heaven," but, "How can we bring the conditions of heaven into our world?" The fascination of a soon coming Jesus to fix the world has caused great harm to the church. It is time for a renewed study of the New Testament, viewing it as the apostolic witness to the arrival of God's kingdom on earth.

For decades I have studied and taught on the present reality of the Kingdom of God. My assignment was and still is to build a theological foundation for hope. Just using 'kingdom words' is not enough; we must have a solid revelation from the Holy Spirit, or else, in days of confusion and negative world events, we will return to our dispensational foundation, which denies God's victory in our time.

Zechariah 1:17

Cry out again, Thus says the LORD of hosts: My cities shall again overflow with prosperity, and the LORD will again comfort Zion and again choose Jerusalem.'"

It is these kinds of promises concerning Israel that kept the dream alive. God will comfort Israel and confirm his favorite status over her. How did this play out? Even after hundreds of years, in the first

---

[84] William B. Nelson Jr., Bakers Evangelical Dictionary of Theology, Bakers Academic, Grand Rapids, Michigan, 1984

century, there were those believing that their God would come and give comfort to Israel.

Luke 2:25-26

Now there was a man in Jerusalem, whose name was Simeon, and this man was righteous and devout, waiting for the consolation of Israel, and the Holy Spirit was upon him. And it had been revealed to him by the Holy Spirit that he would not see death before he had seen the Lord's Christ.

How was the prophecy fulfilled? By the birth of Jesus. This was the comfort Israel and Jerusalem were waiting for. Yet, how did Jesus bring about this comfort? It was not by blessing their present status of being a covenant people. The *"comfort"* of Israel was the better covenant being established by God's Messiah. Those accepting this new world order received comfort and those refusing Jesus, were not comforted, or validated. The Israel that received the *"comfort"* was not ethnic Israel of the old covenant but the true Israel of God - the church.

The Kingdom of God will bring comfort and prosperity to the nations.

47. Zechariah 2:10-11

Sing and rejoice, O daughter of Zion, for behold, I come and I will dwell in your midst, declares the LORD. And many nations shall join themselves to the LORD in that day, and shall be my people. And I will dwell in your midst, and you shall know that the LORD of hosts has sent me to you.

This is the work of Christ in the new covenant. Jeremiah told us of a day, in which God would give Israel and Judah a new covenant, and *"I will be their God, and they will be my people* (Jeremiah 30:31)." This is the day, when all nations would be welcomed into the kingdom. We are long past the time when God favors one nation or people or language over another. God has come and renewed Israel by sending his Messiah. Now every believer, no matter what nationality, is accepted into the family of God. What can we expect in the future? We will see nation after nation bow before the king and great numbers of peoples be joined to God.

"The Kingdom of God, instead of being confined to Israel, will be enlarged by the reception of numerous heathen peoples (Zechariah 8:20, 21; Isaiah 2:3, 16:1; Micah 4:2)."[85]

The promise about God's presence with his people has a larger audience than the nation of Israel. "This was fulfilled in part to the Jews, but more fully to the gospel church."[86] Today, because we have been given the Holy Spirit, our experience of God being with us is greatly enhanced.

As we take the message of the kingdom to the nations, we must carry the 'Presence' of the Kingdom.

48. Zechariah 6:9-13

And the word of the LORD came to me: "Take from the exiles Heldai, Tobijah, and Jedaiah, who have arrived from Babylon, and go the same day to the house of Josiah, the son of Zephaniah. Take from them silver and gold, and make a crown, and set it on the head of Joshua, the son of Jehozadak, the high priest. And say to him, 'Thus says the LORD of hosts, "Behold, the man whose name is the Branch: for he shall branch out from his place, and he shall build the temple of the LORD. It is he who shall build the temple of the LORD and shall bear royal honor, and shall sit and rule on his throne. And there shall be a priest on his throne, and the counsel of peace shall be between them both."

I wish this passage was easier to understand. When I read it there is a sense that the words and symbolism have a depth beyond the first reading. From this single passage, I would think, there could be at least 50 pages of exegesis. Here I would like to point out its

---

[85] John Peter Lange, Lange Commentary on the Holy Scriptures, Zondervan, 1960

[86] Joseph Benson, Benson's Commentary, G. Lane & C.B. Tippett, 1846

relationship to the ongoing kingdom we are living in, but a little history is needed first.

We see the Prophet make a crown and set it upon the head of the high priest. Ezekiel tells us of an event, when the crown was removed.

Ezekiel 21:25-27

And you, O profane wicked one, prince of Israel, whose day has come, the time of your final punishment, thus says the Lord GOD: Remove the turban and take off the crown. Things shall not remain as they are. Exalt that which is low, and bring low that which is exalted. A ruin, ruin, ruin I will make it. This also shall not be, until he comes, the one to whom judgment belongs, and I will give it to him.

Who is this *'prince of Israel'*, that Ezekiel tells to *'take off the crown?'* It is King Zedekiah, who was the final king of Judah. What is left of the covenant nation of Israel (the 10 tribes had already been taken captive and assimilated in their captive nations) is now losing God's authority to rule. Those wanting the story of Zedekiah can read it in II Kings 24-25. Here is the shorter version in II Chronicles.

II Chronicles 36:11-14

Zedekiah was twenty-one years old when he began to reign, and he reigned eleven years in Jerusalem. He did what was evil in the sight of the LORD his God. He did not humble himself before Jeremiah the prophet, who spoke from the mouth of the LORD. He also rebelled against King Nebuchadnezzar, who had made him swear by God. He stiffened his neck and hardened his heart against turning to the LORD, the God of Israel. All the officers of the priests and the people likewise were exceedingly unfaithful, following all the abominations of the nations; and polluted the house of the Lord which he had hallowed in Jerusalem.

Ezekiel is told by God to approach Zedekiah and commands him to take off the crown, because *"Things shall not remain as they are."* God is patient, yet at times he comes and puts an end to things. God is about to show a new way forward. Enough of these wicked kings; there needs to be permanent change and solution to these successive unfaithful kings. And this is what Zechariah is about to symbolically show. A different type of King now receives the crown.

The Babylonian captivity has ended, and various groups have returned to Jerusalem. Zechariah is told to find three such men, receive gifts from them and go to the house of Josiah. There he is to make a crown from the silver and gold, received from the men.

Who receives the crown? It is *"Joshua, the son of Jehozadak, the high priest."*

Barnes: "Zechariah, by placing the royal crown on the head of Joshua, foreshowed that the kingdom was not to be of this world. The royal crown had been taken away in the time of Zedekiah…But the Messiah, it was foretold, was to be both priest and king; "a priest after the order of Melchizedec" Psalm 110:4, and a king, set by the Lord "upon His holy hill of Zion" Psalm 2:6. The act of placing the crown on the head of Joshua the high priest, pictured not only the union of the offices of priest and king in the person of Christ, but that He should be King, being first our High Priest."[87]

We have a symbolic act, that points to the future of who will be both priest and king - Jesus the Christ. What does the Prophet speak after placing the crown? *"Behold the man whose name is The BRANCH; and he shall grow up out of his place, and he shall build the temple of the LORD."*

He may have been looking at Josiah, but the Prophet was looking with hope to the future, when God would bring forth the real priest and king who would build the type of temple God has desired all along.

He calls him the "Branch."

---

[87] Albert Barnes, Barnes Notes on the Old and New Testament, Baker Books, 1983

Jeremiah 33:14-15

*Behold, the days are coming, declares the L*ORD*, when I will fulfill the promise I made to the house of Israel and the house of Judah. In those days and at that time I will cause a righteous Branch to spring up for David, and he shall execute justice and righteousness in the land.*

The name "Branch" is a prophetic word for the Messiah. What will he do that is so vital for Israel and the people of God? He will build *'the temple of the Lord.'*

Jesus never came to solicit support for the physical temple in Jerusalem. He did the opposite. He prophesied its destruction and said it would be left without any purpose.

Matthew 23:37-38

O Jerusalem, Jerusalem, the city that kills the prophets and stones those who are sent to it! How often would I have gathered your children together as a hen gathers her brood under her wings, and you were not willing! See, your house is left to you desolate.

If Jesus had little use for a physical temple what kind of temple did he build?

Ephesians 2:20-21

So then you are no longer strangers and aliens, but you are fellow citizens with the saints and members of the household of God, built on the foundation of the apostles and prophets, Christ Jesus himself being the cornerstone, in whom the whole structure, being joined together, grows into a holy temple in the Lord. In him you also are being built together into a dwelling place for God by the Spirit.

Jesus did establish a temple, not made with stones but out of the living stones of his followers. This glorious temple will be more magnificent and more glorious, having more purpose than any previous temple.

There are many other trails of discovery available in this passage from Zechariah. Like the role of joining and making peace between the divine and human governments. We could ask the difficult question of who is sitting on the throne? Is it one or two people? I think enough has been said to show that seeing these verses through a 'Christocentric' lens is the only way we can see the depth of meaning within this prophecy.

Jesus continues to build his temple in the earth; it is the dwelling place of God, where heaven meets earth.

49. Zechariah 9:9-10

Rejoice greatly, O daughter of Zion!
Shout aloud, O daughter of Jerusalem!
Behold, your king is coming to you;
righteous and having salvation is he,
humble and mounted on a donkey,
on a colt, the foal of a donkey.
I will cut off the chariot from Ephraim
and the war horse from Jerusalem;
and the battle bow shall be cut off,
and he shall speak peace to the nations;
his rule shall be from sea to sea,
and from the River to the ends of the earth.

This passage contains a prophecy about Jesus. It is accurate and points to the actual events in the life of Jesus. Prophecy is supernatural. It reveals that our God knows the future. "The past fulfilment of prophecy should establish our "faith in God" regarding all that is yet future."[88]

Matthew Henry (1662–1714), the non-conformist English minister, wrote about the "*war horse from Jerusalem*" being cut off:

"His kingdom is here set forth in the glory of it. This king has, and will have, a kingdom, not of this world, but a spiritual kingdom, a kingdom of heaven. It shall not be set up and advanced by external

---

[88] Ralph Wardlaw, Bible Illustrator, https://biblehub.com/commentaries/illustrator/zechariah/9.htm

force, by an arm of flesh or carnal weapons of warfare. No; he will cut off the chariot from Ephraim and the horses from Jerusalem (v. 10), for he shall have no occasion for them while he himself rides upon an ass. He will, in kindness to his people, cut off their horses and chariots, that they may not cut themselves off from God by putting that confidence in them which they should put in the power of God only. He will himself undertake their protection, will himself be a wall of fire about Jerusalem and give his angels charge concerning it."[89]

Israel, your King is coming to you. The question to the generation that saw the fulfillment of this prophecy is, "Will you receive him?" We know from history that as a nation, Israel rejected their Messiah (John 1:11). Yet, according to Apostle Paul, God has not rejected Israel, because he and other members of this *'remnant of Israel'* received King Jesus. Now we who are Gentiles are added into this rich root of promises and are connected to the king of the world.

For those who see the kingdom of God being established through the ministry of Jesus in the first century and advancing since then; there is no large gap in time from when he rode into Jerusalem and his coronation as King. The dispensational approach must inject into this passage a gap of time to match their theology. They agree that the first part of the prophecy was fulfilled in the first century, but Zechariah saw a 2,000-year gap of time (and growing) from his entrance into Jerusalem, to the time which he rules as King over the nations. This, they will demand takes place after the Second Coming in their version of the Millennium. I believe Zechariah had it right. Jesus came as King and is now reigning as King. I do not see evidence for any time gap, either in the Old Testament and especially in the New Testament where the kingdom of God was not 'far off', but 'at hand' and was preached by Jesus and his Apostles.

---

[89] Matthew Henry, Matthew Henry's Commentary on the Whole Bible, Hendrickson Publishers, Box Una Edition, 2009

What is the message of the king? *"He shall speak peace to the nations."* We, in the church, cannot allow our priorities to be any different than our king.

In the modern world of Evangelicals, those who work towards peace are viewed with suspicion. We question whether their politics are conservative. Over the centuries the church resisted war whenever possible. Yet, today, when a governmental leader needs public support for a war, it is the Evangelicals who are among the first to support the cause.

Theology cannot be divorced from our position concerning war and military conflict. The dispensationalists believe world conditions must get worse because they embrace the doctrine that we live in the *'last days'* and Jesus will soon 'rapture' us out of this evil world. That's why their ideology that supports military conflicts is easy. Wars for them means 'Jesus is coming soon.' For those of us who embrace a victorious eschatology and an advancement of the kingdom of peace in the nations, 'war' should be a difficult decision. Since King Jesus is the prince of peace, we should follow his example.

The Church needs to be the voice of peace in the world.

50. Malachi 4:4-6

Remember the law of my servant Moses, the statutes and rules that I commanded him at Horeb for all Israel. "Behold, I will send you Elijah the prophet before the great and awesome day of the LORD comes. And he will turn the hearts of fathers to their children and the hearts of children to their fathers, lest I come and strike the land with a decree of utter destruction."

We cannot get around the fact that the Old Testament age was about the Law of Moses. The Law was the standard. It was the people's morality. It was how they knew right from wrong. It was how they worshipped. It was everything. No wonder there remain theologians who claim God wants to re-instate the old law in the future. Now, here at the end of the Old Testament the prophet reminds the struggling and rebellious people to remember the Law of Moses.

The Prophet reminds everyone to remember the law of Moses and then a huge transition takes place. He jumps from the present time and takes his readers 400 years in the future. *"Behold, I will send you Elijah."* What is that about? Despite the dire circumstances of Malachi's day; hope is on the way. Something is coming, which would change everything. And it would be big!

The prophecy is not just about Elijah and his restorative ministry; it is much larger than that. The appearance of Elijah will open the door to the *"Great and awesome Day of the Lord."*

If you are among some of the extreme folks out there, who believe this prophecy remains unfulfilled and you are still looking for Elijah, I cannot help you. There is an abundance of material by respected scholars that outlines how John the Baptist fulfilled this prophecy. I recommend you study them. What needs to be viewed more in depth is the subject of the *'Day of the Lord.'*

The *"Day of the Lord'* began in the garden of Eden, where the first day took place. The day separates us from the darkness. Entering the kingdom of God is a step into the *'Day.'* It is a time of 'seeing' and of 'revelation' through the Spirit. Beyond the positive elements of the 'Day' is also a season of judgment.

Let's begin with the words of John the Baptist.

Matthew 3:7-11

But when he saw many of the Pharisees and Sadducees coming to his baptism, he said to them, "You brood of vipers! Who warned you to flee from the wrath to come? Bear fruit in keeping with repentance. And do not presume to say to yourselves, 'We have Abraham as our father,' for I tell you, God is able from these stones to raise up children for Abraham. Even now the axe is laid to the root of the trees. Every tree therefore that does not bear good fruit is cut down and thrown into the fire. "I baptize you with water for repentance, but he who is coming after me is mightier than I, whose sandals I am not worthy to carry. He will baptize you with the Holy Spirit and fire."

In this passage John the Baptist covered key areas of the transition about to take place. He foretold the coming judgment upon old covenant Israel. The Baptist goes right to the issue - the leaders of Israel loved to play the religious role, but their hearts proved by the lack of any character (lack of fruit), they were already hardened to the one he was introducing. They would face the *'wrath to come.'*

The final words in the Old Testament, found in Malachi are, *"Lest I come and strike the land with a decree of utter destruction."* Malachi had a word for the future first-century religious leaders and their followers, that they would witness the destruction of their land.

Malachi spoke to a people not born for another 400 years. Whether the Prophet knew this or not, no one can be sure. At times the Prophets would use the words, the *'latter days,'* or speak of the coming Messiah, but most times we are left without any help as to the time of its fulfillment. Looking backwards is always easier than forward, even for Prophets.

Once we learn the 'Apostolic Hermeneutic' we can partake deeply from the rich root of the olive tree.

Books by Stan Newton

Glorious Kingdom

A Handbook on Partial Preterist Eschatology

Glorious Kingdom is a comprehensive book on eschatology; kingdom eschatology. In this book Stan Newton takes on dispensational eschatology, which is the position of many evangelicals, and lays a foundation from Scripture for a different view. Glorious Kingdom covers all major aspects of eschatology with special emphasis on interpreting the prophetic New Testament passages from the viewpoint of the kingdom of God. The kingdom was established by Jesus in the first century. This book will help those seeking biblical answers to tough questions on eschatology.

Glorious Covenant

Our Journey Toward Better Covenant Theology

God is a God of covenants. Christians have a covenant. With these two basic foundations Stan Newton compares contemporary views of covenant. He examines Dispensationalism, Covenant Theology and New Covenant Theology. Glorious Covenant finds the fault lines of each position and then through Scriptural discovery argues for a fourth view; Better Covenant Theology. Sadly, many Christians are only vaguely aware of this glorious covenant. How followers of Jesus understand covenant is extremely important and Glorious Covenant pushes away the confusion and presents a clear view of the New Covenant we have in Christ.

Kingdom Communion

The Mystery of the Fourth Cup

Kingdom Communion is written with the conviction that the Lord's Supper must return to its proper place in our regular worship services. Too many churches have forgotten the table of the Lord.

Is it because our 'communion service' is more like a funeral than a wedding? Stan Newton addresses the historical beliefs and then offers something different; viewing communion from a kingdom and eschatological position. When Jesus as the 'Son of man' came in his kingdom to end one age and begin a new age-the kingdom age-then, our understanding of communion must change. When will Jesus drink the fourth cup with us?

Breakfast in Tel Aviv

A Conversation About Israel

Theological Fiction

Shane recently graduated from a Pentecostal Bible School. His future was secure within his denomination, except for one thing; he changed his theology. Breakfast in Tel Aviv is the story of two Pastors as they discuss the end times and Israel. Emotions are high as they discuss their views. Their discussions lead to a trip to Israel and over breakfast all is resolved; or is it?

King First (3 Volumes)

Bible Studies for the Kingdom/New Covenant Church

Stan Newton has taken the major themes of his books, Glorious Kingdom and Glorious Covenant and created a three-volume Bible Study. These Kingdom lessons will assist home groups, Sunday school classes, discipleship classes, as well as individuals in learning the great biblical truths concerning the Kingdom of God and New Covenant living.

All Books Available on Amazon

Kingdom Missions:
The Ministry of Stan and Virginia Newton

We are singularly focused on teaching and demonstrating the Gospel of the Kingdom as taught in Stan's book, <u>Glorious Kingdom</u>. Through Seminars/Bible Schools/Churches we present the view of Christ's present and advancing Kingdom. Virginia specializes in literacy where she travels with a team to other nations and prepares teaching manuals so those unable to read the language may learn. The manuals they prepare use a biblical curriculum that leads them to the study of Jesus. Stan and Virginia are based in Sofia, Bulgaria and speak throughout Europe and in the United States.

We need your help in taking this message to the nations. You can E-mail us at <u>svnewton@hotmail.com</u> or become a friend on Facebook. To send letters or financial gifts please mail to Kingdom Missions PO Box 948 Seattle, WA. 98111